NOBODY READS

LEVITICUS

By the same author

Today We Encounter a Hard Saying

FR. IVOR KRAFT

NOBODY READS LEVITICUS

More Sermons by the Sea

Nobody Reads Leviticus is a collection of sixteen sermons
given by Fr. H. Ivor Kraft from 2007 to 2014 at
St. Michael's by-the-Sea Episcopal Church
in Carlsbad, California USA

Sermons 1-9 and 11-16 transcribed by Craig Klampe
Other material surreptitiously recorded by Chucho

Cover Art
Temptation of Christ (mosaic in the Basilica di San Marco)
Courtesy of http://en.wikipedia.org

Printed by CreateSpace, An Amazon.com Company
Source audio is available at stmichaelsbythesea.org

I would speak to many souls,
but the world keeps up such a noise about their ears
that My voice would never be heard by them.
Oh, that they would retire a little from the world!

Jesus to St. Teresa of Ávila

CONTENTS

Introduction · 9

PART I: OBEDIENCE

    Nobody Reads Leviticus · 13

1   Ears Are For Hearing · 15

2   Saved and Savior · 23

3   Called to Suffer? · 29

4   That's Nice · 38

PART II: SIMPLICITY

    The Twist · 47

5   So Complicated! · 49

6   What Is Enough? · 54

7   On a Journey · 62

8   Nice v. Good · 70

PART III: FAITH

    The Liberation of Fr. Ivor · 79

9   Gypsies and Heretics · 81

10   The Power to Explain Nothing · 88

11   Concealed and Revealed · 94

12   Getting the Picture · 101

PART IV: PERSEVERANCE

    It's Happening Again · 111

13   The Usual Advice · 117

14   Food for the Journey · 127

15   All the Difference in the World · 135

16   God Bless St. Michael's · 143

APPENDIX

    Prayer · 155

INTRODUCTION

Dear Padre -

Let me introduce you to your own book. You'd think that the second collection of your sermons would be like the first and therefore need no introduction. Little do you know! You see, not only are there sermons transcribed here, but there are a few passages overheard by my Moto X at Rubio's and even a moment from evening prayer. I didn't tell you ahead of time because I didn't know if it could work. Now it's time for you to tell me if it does. What do you think? (You are sitting down, right?) I know you've been waiting for People Magazine to call. Ken Burns perhaps? No worries! Until then, your public can have a sampling of Fr. Ivor away from the pulpit. Or, as Fr. Doran might put it: Here is Fr. Ivor Unplugged.

Chucho*
The Feast of St. Teresa of Ávila
October 15, 2014

---

* At the behest of Fr. Ivor, who was sitting down, I will explain who Chucho is. In seventh grade Spanish class, we students were given Spanish names and "Craig" became "Chucho." I use this name to distinguish myself from all the other Craigs when ordering at the local Mexican food hangout, even though my credit card does say "Craig Klampe, transcriber and editor of Fr. Ivor books." Fr. Ivor didn't behest me to explain who "Padre" is, because Padre is a man beyond explanation.

PART I

Obedience

Nobody Reads Leviticus

Nobody ever speaks about Leviticus. I mentioned that to my homiletics class. One of my students brought up, "Father forgive them for they know not what they do." And I said, "And that brings us to Leviticus!"

Nobody ever reads Leviticus. Leviticus is a very, very important book of the Bible and if you read Leviticus you will find out that God established a sacrificial system so that Israel will have something to offer to Him because we need to offer and God said He would condescend to accept this stuff which He didn't need and didn't want but that Israel needed to offer. And He would accept it as a sacrifice for unwitting sin. And that there was no sacrifice for "sin with a high hand," only for unwitting sins. Therefore our Lord, the climactic and fulfilling sacrifice that ends all sacrifice, can pray for those who are doing that which they know not what they do, who are in other words not sinning with a high hand.

But people know not what I am talking about because they do not read Leviticus.

1

Ears Are For Hearing

In the name of the Father and of the Son
and of the Holy Spirit.

The annual diocesan convention was held this week on Friday and Saturday and it reminded me of an experience I had at a convention twenty-five or thirty years ago. As is the custom at these events, there are workshops. Although I've forgotten most of them, one has always stuck in my mind. I can't remember the point that the leader was trying to make, but I do remember what I took away. This is what happened.

Fifty or sixty of us gathered in a large room. And the leader handed out a sheet of paper containing a list of ten items. He then asked us to check the things on the list that were essential as opposed to those things on the list that were desirable, to distinguish the essential from the desirable.

I scanned the list and I remember that it contained among other things, among the things that I can't remember any more, a car, a university education, a television set, and other such accoutrements of middle class life. But in the middle... (and by the way I should probably say today, if this was being done today, it would have to have on there a computer and that without which man cannot live: the smartphone. Talk about essential! Right? In any event...) In the middle of the list, sticking out, it was to me like the proverbial sore thumb, was a year's supply of vegetables.

This, I thought to myself, is too easy. A year's supply of vegetables. Food! Food is the only essential thing on this list, really. My parents left school, both of them, at the end of eighth grade and went to work full time. They lived very well without benefit of a university education. I managed to get to be twenty-two without a car. Hated it. I wish (I wish!) I didn't have a television. That's not an essential or a luxury: it's an affliction. So anyway, I checked off "a year's supply of vegetables" and I waited to see where the whole thing was going.

Predictably, we were asked to form groups, groups in this case of eight, and share. You always have to share, you know? You can't avoid it ever! To my dismay, a dismay that's lasted to this day, I discovered that I alone had checked "a year's supply of vegetables" as the one essential on the list. And I found myself trying to explain why a university education or a television set might be desirable but were certainly not essential to life. It was a losing battle. I convinced no one.

Perhaps the problem was that I grew up in Pittsburgh where even today, much less then, university graduates form a small minority. As opposed to Mission Viejo where the only people without a university degree are the gardeners. Right? And that's not a wisecrack at the expense of people in Mission Viejo. I live in a community just like that. It's an observation about how our perceptions are formed by our surroundings, by the people who live around us, by the community that we are raised in.

I'm also not claiming that I was the only person at the workshop who "saw the light." Far from it. But I did come away filled with the conviction that we all need to think deeply about the distinction between the necessary and the desirable. What I want and what I need, really are more often than not, two different things. And wisdom is found in being able to make the proper distinctions. Desire is limitless! It knows no end and often runs contrary to need altogether.

To do the things that I am required to do, I need an automobile. As it happens, I have a very nice automobile. I have a Toyota; that's what I have. What I want is an Aston Martin. I want that car that James Bond had (the real James Bond, not the impersonators who came after). He had that Aston Martin that I've wanted for what? … more years than

I care to remember. Let's just leave it at that. But of course I need an Aston Martin like I need a hole in the head. Right? The oil changes and the tune-ups would probably bankrupt me, not to mention the insurance! I don't want to think about it. But I still, as I'm there on the freeway — becalmed on Route 5 — wish I were sitting in that car. Right? Of course, if I had that car, it would spend a lot of time in the garage and I'd have to borrow Fr. Doran's Toyota.

In case you're wondering where this is all going, in case you're wondering, saying to yourself, "Well, you know, Father, it's interesting that you covet an Aston Martin but what does that have to do with the word of God for us?" Well, we're coming to that.

In today's Gospel, our Lord encounters a man with leprosy who begs Him for help.

> A leper came to Jesus beseeching Him and kneeling said to Him, If You will, You can make me clean. (Mk 1:40)

Leprosy, aside from all the terrible physical effects of the disease, also involved ritual uncleanness and complete segregation from the community of Israel and its religious life. In other words, the leper was strictly quarantined, as anyone with an infectious and terrible disease should be. The law, the law of Moses found in the book of Leviticus, tells you all about this, all about how Israel was to deal with the leper. The law could not heal the leper; it could only protect the rest of the community from him.

The leper in today's Gospel is the very image of the man at prayer in the presence of God. What the laws can't help us to do, is possible with God, and so he kneels before the Lord beseeching His help.

> Moved with pity, the Lord stretched out His hand and touched him. (Mk 1:41)

It would be easy to overlook this act of our Lord, that He reached out and touched the leper. But this is one of the three things forbidden by Mosaic legislation. You cannot touch the leper, you cannot touch a woman with a hemorrhage, you cannot touch a corpse without incurring ritual uncleanness. And the Lord touched all three, St. Mark tells us. And by doing so He was, in each case, manifesting His identity. What no man can do, God can do. What man must not or should not touch — that is, heal — God can heal.

According to the British scholar D. E. Nineham, "the rabbis of our Lord's time believed healing leprosy was as difficult as raising the dead." As difficult as raising the dead. Nineham also remarks that there is some evidence to suggest that the cleansing of leprosy was an expected sign of the Messiah's arrival, and therefore that our Lord's ability to cleanse the leper is again a manifestation of His identity as the Messiah. "Moved with pity, the Lord stretched out His hand and touched him. 'I will make you clean,' the Lord said. 'Be clean.'"

What no man can do, God can do. The Lord can cleanse and restore the leper to his home and to his community. Today's psalm is relevant here. And I would hope that the leper, an Israelite, prayed these words when the Lord cleansed him. (Ps 30:2,3)

> O Lord my God, I cried out to You,
> and You restored me to health.
> You brought me up, O Lord, from the dead.
> You restored my life
> as I was going down to the grave.

The Lord Who broke the law about not touching the leper was clearly not disdainful of the law. After all, He was ultimately the author of the law of Moses. Therefore He commanded the leper, now cleansed, to show himself to the priest and "offer for your cleansing what Moses commanded for a proof to the people."

But before sending the leper to the priest to offer sacrifice and be declared clean publicly before the community so that he could be restored to his home and his family and his life, to his world, the Lord "sternly" (and mark that word "sternly")… the Lord

> sternly charged him and sent him away at once and
> said to him, See that you say nothing to anyone. But
> he went out and began to talk freely about it and to
> spread the news. (Mk 1:43-45)

The Lord, moved with pity, listened to the man. The man, having received that which he desired, would not listen to the Lord. The man thought he needed to be cleansed of his leprosy. What the leper needed were ears with which to hear the Lord, Who had listened to him and Who had had pity on him. The man's problem was not his leprosy but his deafness. The man had ears but he would not hear, that is, he would not obey. He received from the Lord what he wanted but not what he needed. It is not his leprosy but his deafness to the Lord which is, in the words of St. Paul, his "sickness unto death."

The leper cleansed was restored to his community but turned his back on God. He gained the world but, in our Lord's words, he lost his soul. (Mk 8:36) When we hear that the leper went out and began to talk freely about what the Lord had done for him, we are all too easily seduced into believing that was a good thing, and it's not. It was an act of disobedience, explicit disobedience to the Lord Who had charged him not casually but sternly to say nothing. This, this is a symptom of the universal malady of the human race. We know what we want, but all too rarely do we know what we need. What we need above all is God Himself, and therefore ears with which to hear Him when He speaks to us. This is what our Lord Himself called, in His conversation with Martha and Mary of Bethany, the one thing needful. (Lk 10:42) And therefore may each of us and all of us pray fervently, pray like that man with leprosy calling out to the Lord, for ears with which to hear Him when He speaks to us.

Amen.

2

Saved and Savior

In the name of the Father, and of the Son,
and of the Holy Spirit.

When our Lord was baptized by John, the heavenly voice declared, "This is My beloved Son with Whom I am well pleased." (Mt 3:17) These words of God identified Jesus and, for reasons that there is no time to go into this morning, also defined and announced His mission, which was to bear the cross. The evangelists tell us that immediately after His baptism and this announcement, that Jesus was led up by the Spirit into the wilderness to be tempted by the devil. And each year on the first Sunday in Lent, the Church reads the narrative of our Lord's temptation in the wilderness. You may remember the devil's taunts.

If you are the Son of God, turn these stones into loaves
of bread. (Mt 4:3) Everyone's hungry, the world is a

hungry place, and bread is a symbol of all material need and necessity. Feed everybody and they will all flock to you.

If you are the Son of God, throw yourself down from the pinnacle of the Temple and let God's holy angels rescue you. (Mt 4:6) Now that's a persuasive miracle, a sign, and people love spectacle and they love miracles and if you perform miracles and signs they will flock to you.

If you are really the Son of God, become ruler of the world! (Mt 4:8-9) After all, the world's rulers are a bad lot, generation after generation. And you would be the perfect ruler of the world, the perfectly good king.

If you are really the Son of God, why do something as futile and useless as bearing the cross? If you are really the Son of God, you can do anything you please. So do something useful, why don't you?

Our Lord resisted these temptations, but the enemy is ever active and has one goal. The enemy has only one goal, and that's to separate us from God by any means possible and available. In the case of our Lord Jesus Christ Himself, this meant separating Him from His cross. And in the passion narrative, the deceiver and the father of lies returns for one last chance to separate our Lord from His cross, speaking through those who surround the Lord at His crucifixion. Hear the voice of the tempter.

Those who passed by derided Him, wagging their heads and saying, You who would destroy the Temple and build it in three days, save yourself. If you are the Son of God, come down from the cross. (Mt 27:39-40)

So also the chief priests with the scribes and the elders mocked Him saying, He saved others; He cannot save Himself. He's the King of Israel! (That is to say, the Lord God.) Let Him come down now from the cross and we will believe in him. He trusts in God, let God deliver him now, if he desires him, for he said, I am the Son of God. (Mt 27: 41-43)

And the robbers who were also crucified with Him reviled Him in the same way. If you're really the son of God, save yourself. Come down from the cross, and we will believe in you. (Mt 27:44)

The temptation is the same temptation that the Lord encountered in the wilderness. Jesus is being tempted to take things into His Own hands rather than trust in the One Who promised to raise Him on the third day and vindicate Him. Just as in the wilderness, when He was urged to draw all men to Himself through spectacle and miracle, He is now urged to do the same by using His divine power (if He really has any) to come down from the cross. 'Do this and we will believe in you. Act like a king, behave like a god, manifest your power, and we'll follow you.'

But our Lord's saving work and divine calling was to perform an act of trusting love and loving trust. Remember, our Lord teaches clearly that to love God means to obey Him.

> I do as the Father has commanded me so that the world may know that I love the Father. (Jn 14:31)

Or as we heard in the Epistle:

> Though He was in the form of God, He did not count equality with God a thing to be grasped but emptied Himself, taking the form of a servant, being found in the likeness of men, and being found in human form, He humbled Himself and became obedient unto death, even death on a cross. (Phil 2:6-8)

In the Garden of Eden, Adam—wanting to be like God rather than serve Him as His creature—believed the tempter; and rather than trust God, he took things into His own hands with disastrous results for all of us, past, present, and future. In the garden of Gethsemane, Jesus Himself prayed, "Father, if it be possible, let this cup pass from Me, yet not My will but Your will be done." (Mt 26:39)

Jesus was asked to trust God even unto death on the cross. He came into the world not to do His Own will, but the will of the One Who sent Him. He was not sent to take matters into His Own hands. He was not sent to save Himself. Rather, He came into the world to cast Himself heart, mind, soul, and body, from the arms of the cross into the arms of the God He called 'Father.' He did not come to save Himself but to be saved, and having been saved, to become our savior.

We too, whether we realize it or not, or wish to acknowledge it or not, are constantly plagued by the tempter. And our temptation is to hear the passion narratives of our Lord's suffering and death as a sad, sorrowful tragedy, as a defeat. The enemy was unable to separate the Lord from His cross. And so now, all he can do is try to get us to see our Lord's suffering and death as some kind of sad defeat.

But by succumbing to this temptation, we join the company of all those who mocked and derided Him, and who did believe that they had defeated Him. Our Lord's refusal to allow anyone or anything, including Peter and the Apostles, to separate Him from His cross, is His glory. And because this is so, the Church has proclaimed through the centuries that through the cross, joy came into the world. Our Lord is proclaiming to us by word and deed from the cross, that nothing can surpass an act of humble obedience to God performed out of love for Him.

Don't be deceived by the deceiver. The death of our Lord Jesus Christ is not a defeat. It is His victory, a victory that at last enables us to see the face of God in the face of Jesus. And so it was that the centurion, at the death of our Lord, does not see Him as a defeated individual but is able to say, "Truly, this was the Son of God." (Mt 27:54)

Amen.

3

Called to Suffer?

From that time, Jesus began to show His disciples that
He must go to Jerusalem and suffer many things from
the elders and the chief priests and scribes and be killed,
and on the third day be raised.

Mt 16:21

I feel compelled to begin by saying that Christianity is not
a cult of suffering. And I begin by saying that because, in
light of what we've just heard, it would be possible to believe
that it is.

What our Lord does, and did, is turn all religious
teaching on its head. Hans Urs von Balthasar, the great Swiss
theologian, put it this way. "The Church consists of people,
all of whom wish to escape suffering as much and as long
as possible. All religions outside of Christianity respond in
some way to this plan—how can a man flee suffering?"

I believe this is true, but I don't believe that von

Balthasar goes far enough. The real problem is not simply suffering but innocent suffering. Innocent suffering is a moral offense. And if religion presents plans to flee from suffering, it also seeks to explain innocent suffering by denying that it exists. The great religions of the world deny that there is any such thing as innocent suffering. This was, and I believe is still true of Judaism.

The Lord God had made it clear to Israel that if she kept the covenant that He had made with her, that she would prosper. If she violated the covenant and fell into idolatry, she would suffer.

The story of ancient Israel, her victories and defeats, her joys and sufferings, is the story of her alternating fidelity and infidelity. And in periods of fidelity to the Lord, she prospers, and when she turns away from the Lord into the worship of idols and into evil, the Lord brings wrath upon her. But questions arose in ancient Israel as they do always. Experience teaches that sometimes those who are faithful to the Lord suffer, and this raises the question, "Why?"

In today's first reading, we heard the prayer of the prophet Jeremiah. The 'thees' and the 'thous' make it a little difficult to follow, but I want to read part of it to you.

> O Lord, Thou knowest;
> remember me and visit me,
> and take vengeance for me on my persecutors. (Jer 15:15)

Jeremiah was given a word by the Lord to speak to Israel, an Israel that had fallen into idolatry and every evil, and the Israelites resented it terribly and they hated Jeremiah for speaking the word of the Lord to them. And so they persecuted him.

> In Thy forbearance take me not away.
>> Know that for Your sake I bear reproach.
> Your words were found, and I ate them,
>> and Your words became to me a joy
>> and the delight of my heart,
> for I am called by Your name,
>> O Lord, God of hosts.

> I did not sit in the company of merrymakers,
>> nor did I rejoice.
> I sat alone because Your hand was upon me,
>> for You had filled me with indignation.

> Why is my pain unceasing
>> and my wound incurable,
>> refusing to be healed?
>
> Jer 15:15-18

"When I found Your words, I ate them." That's a description of the prophetic vocation: the prophet receives a word from the Lord and eats it. And then is called upon to repeat it. "When I found Your words I ate them and they became my joy and the happiness of my heart for I bore Your name, O Lord God of hosts. Why then is my pain unceasing, my wound incurable?"

The prophet Habakkuk asked a related question. In the time of the Babylonian ascendancy, when they were overwhelming Israel, he asked,

Why Lord are you silent when the wicked swallows up
the man more righteous than he? (Hab 1:13)

Here we have the question of relative innocence. Habakkuk didn't claim that Israel was all that faithful, but they certainly were not as evil as the Chaldeans.

And of course there's Job, the old testament innocent sufferer par excellence. Job asked "Why?" and his good friends who came to visit him told him, "Well, the answer was simple." The reason he was suffering all those terrible things was because he was a sinner who had transgressed and was suffering his just desert and he should stop complaining (for sixty chapters, hm?) and own up! "You should man up and say to the Lord 'All right, I'm guilty, and I'm getting everything I deserve.'"

But Job refused to do that. Absolutely refused to do it. And that's the drama of the book of Job. He denied that he was guilty of a transgression that deserved all that had befallen him, and finally the Lord intervenes and condemns

Job's friends and tells Job's friends that they're wrong and that Job's right. But he doesn't answer the question, "Why?"

And then in the prophet Isaiah, there are four oracles, four prophetic utterances of the suffering servant of the Lord, a mysterious figure who brings life and forgiveness by his perfectly innocent sufferings. But nobody knew what that meant.

And all of these instances are isolated exceptions in the sacred literature of ancient Israel and the question "Why?" remained unanswered. For Israel, suffering was divine punishment for transgression, and health, wealth, and happiness were the signs of divine love and approval.

The word of the Lord for us today that we heard read from St. Matthew, is the second half of a reading that really can't properly be divided. We heard the first half last Sunday. (Mt 16:13-20) And in case you weren't at Mass last Sunday, or in case you're now searching your memory trying to say, "Yeah, what was that gospel last Sunday anyway?" it is this. (A quick recap for you.)

The Lord takes His apostles and disciples who have been following Him for a year or two, observing Him, listening to Him, learning from Him. He takes them as far away from Jerusalem as He can get to the north, to Caesarea Philippi, and there He asks them, "Who do men say that I am?" And they start, you know, the yada yada, as Jerry Seinfeld says. They say, "Well, some people say, 'Elijah.' Some people say, 'John the Baptist,' or 'Jeremiah,' or one of the other prophets. And then He asks them the great question, the question that you and I also have to answer—if not now, we'll have to answer it on the Day of Judgement—"Who do you say that I am?" And Peter, speaking for the others, says, "You are the Christ, and the Son of the living God." And our Lord says,

> Simon bar Jona, flesh and blood has not revealed this to you, but My Father Who is in heaven. And you are Peter, the Rock, and on this rock I will found My Church and the gates of hell will not prevail against it.

And from that time—and that's really what we should have heard first but if you look in your lectionary they left out those words—from that time—from the time they recognize Him and can identify Him—Jesus began to show His disciples that He must go to Jerusalem and suffer many things from the elders and chief priests. In other words, He does not tell them what His mission is until they know Who He is. And once they recognize Him and know Who He is, then He begins to explain what that means. Because now He's going to turn religion upside down.

From that time (when they finally understood His identity,

when they recognized Him), He began to show His disciples that He must go to Jerusalem and suffer many things from the elders and the chief priests and the scribes and be killed and on the third day raised. And Peter took Him and began to rebuke Him, saying, "God forbid, Lord, that this should ever happen to You."

Well, of course Peter would say that! He was an Israelite. The Messiah, the Anointed One of God and the Son of God, does not suffer. He makes other people suffer. Peter's reaction, his response to the Lord's word of the cross was predictable. But not the Lord's response. (Mt 16:23)

> Get behind me, Satan. You are a hindrance to me, for
> you are not on the side of God but of men.

And here we should remember the temptation in the wilderness when the devil first tried to separate the Lord from His cross. Suddenly the rock on which the Lord said He would build His church, against which not even the gates of hell could prevail, suddenly the rock, Peter, is the devil. Because God the Father had sent His Son into the world to bear the cross, to suffer, die and be raised on the third day. And since this was the Lord's divinely given mission, anyone who would attempt to separate Him from His cross was on the side of the devil, even Peter. Jesus and His cross are inseparable in time and eternity. Christianity is the religion of the crucified God.

Innocent suffering does exist, and we know it because the perfectly innocent One suffered more than anyone before or since. By His cross and passion, the Lord has taken all innocent suffering—yours, mine, and everyone's—into His own innocent suffering in order to heal it and in order to heal us. The crucified Christ and Son of the living God Who so offended Peter because of His willingness to endure the cross continues to offend a world which sees suffering only as negative, only as something to be avoided at all costs. But our Lord is Himself the mysterious servant of God spoken of through the prophet Isaiah Who will bring life and light and hope through His Own innocent sufferings. Jesus the Son of God is God's Own and final answer to Jeremiah, Habakkuk, Job and everyone everywhere who asks, "Why?"

And our Lord tells us that we too must take up our crosses and follow Him, but if we understand the cross to represent suffering, then we will make Christianity a cult of suffering and if we have any brains, we will flee from it.

The historical cross of our Lord was given Him by His Father in heaven, the same Father in heaven Who revealed to Peter that He was the Christ and Son of the living God. The cross is not a symbol of suffering, it is a symbol of divine love. It is a symbol of the Son's love for the Father in the Spirit. It is a symbol and sign of Jesus' perfect love for the God Who sent Him into the world, His perfect conformity to the Father's will.

Our Lord prayed in the garden of Gethsemane as we all know, "My Father, if it be possible, let this cup pass from me. But not My will, Your will be done." (Mt 26:39) Our Lord accepted suffering, He did not desire it. Our Lord was not a masochist, to use the language—right?—of modern psychology. To take up the cross is not to seek suffering, but to adhere to the Lord's will, even when it conflicts with my will, and even when it may lead to unwanted suffering. To take up the cross and find our true lives does not mean seeking suffering but acceptance of suffering should it come to us in our love for and obedience to God.

> If any man would come after Me, let him deny himself and take up his cross and follow Me. For whoever would save his life will lose it, and whoever loses his life for My sake will find it. (Mt 16:24-25)

To surrender our wills to God's will is to lose ourselves. And it is in this losing of ourselves for His sake, that the Lord promises us that we will find ourselves.

Amen.

4

That's Nice

*In the name of the Father and of the Son
and of the Holy Spirit.*

God does not ask me, much less does He command me, to like you. He doesn't ask or command me to like anyone! And that's a very good thing because it means I'm not required to like Fr. Doran who's always making up crazy stories about me!

But I digress.

To like. "To like" means, according to Webster, to get pleasure from something. As in "I like coffee." Or to regard something or someone in a favorable way. Or to feel affection for someone or something. "To like" is about the affections. That is to say, the emotions. But "to love" is about will. "Love your enemies and pray for those who persecute you,"

says the Lord. (Mt 5:44, Lk 6:27) For many years I believed this to be the most impossible of all the commandments given to us by our Lord to observe. You see, I had mistakenly believed that our Lord was asking me to like my enemies, and nothing could be further from the truth.

Our Lord does not ask me or you to like anyone, but commands us to love everyone. If I were to tell our Lord that I like St. Michael's and that I like you (and I do!) I suspect He'd say to me, "That's nice."

Nice is as different from good as like is from love.

I don't know if the Lord likes me, but I'm convinced that He loves me. Not because of any virtue of mine but because He is good. He is absolute goodness.

People are sometimes scandalized by the God of Jesus Christ and by Jesus Himself because they read the Bible looking for a nice God rather than a good God. Around 3,500 years ago, the Lord God led Israel out of Egypt, out of slavery, and He led Israel to the Holy Mountain, to Sinai, and there He gave Israel His commandments. God had proven to the Israelites that He was all-powerful when He defeated the gods of Egypt, and He was in the process of proving that He was trustworthy because He was keeping the promise that He had made to Abraham, Isaac, and Jacob, to give to them and their descendants a land to dwell in. But at Mount Sinai, at the Holy Mountain, He did something every bit as great as all that, and inseparable from Him. The Lord revealed that He is good, not simply all-powerful, not simply trustworthy, but good. He revealed that He is a moral being.

At the Holy Mountain, Moses came before the Israelites and he built an altar of stone with twelve pillars representing the twelve tribes of Israel, and on that altar he sacrificed oxen and he took the blood of the oxen, the life of the oxen, drained it into bowls, and then he read all the words, that is to say all the commandments, of the Lord to the Israelites. And the Israelites responded and said that "all that the Lord has said, we will do, and we will be obedient." And Moses took half the blood of the oxen, of the sacrificial beasts, and he threw it against the altar and the other half he cast onto the Israelites and he said,

> Behold the blood of the covenant which the Lord has made with you this day in accordance with all His commands. (Ex 24:8)

When we hear the word of the Christ today, "All of you drink of this cup, for this cup is the new covenant in my blood," (Lk 22:20) we need to hear the word of Moses, casting the blood of the oxen onto the Israelites and saying, "Behold the blood of the covenant which the Lord has made with you this day." That is precisely the old covenant. You cannot have a new covenant without an old one.

The Lord gave Israel His commandments to reveal

His moral being, His goodness, and to invite Israel to participate, to share in His goodness by observing His commandments. He didn't give Israel the commandments for His good, because we can add nothing to His goodness. He gave Israel the commandments so that by receiving them and observing them, Israel could share in the goodness of God, could participate in His goodness, and be a sign in the midst of all the other nations of the goodness of God.

The only thing that anyone can possess greater than the word of God, greater than the commandments of God, is the author and definitive interpreter of those commandments, that is to say God Himself, Jesus Christ our Lord, which is the One we are here to receive today. In fact, the only thing that God did not give to Israel was Himself. And the climax of everything that God wills to do is to give Himself to us.

The pagan philosopher Aristotle argued that happiness is an activity of the soul in accord with the good. Whatever the disciples of Aristotle may think he means by that, the part that has always interested me is that Aristotle grasped the inseparable connection between happiness and goodness. No goodness, no happiness.

I've been guilty of saying that I just want my children to be happy. But I think I'm mistaken in this. Rémi Brague is a French professor of Arabic and religious philosophy at the

Sorbonne in Paris and a German university in Munich. He is also more importantly — at least to my mind — a Christian, and recently the author of a book titled, *On the God of the Christians (and On One or Two Others)*. It's a slender but profound meditation on the God of Jesus Christ, the Most Holy and Blessed Trinity. The book provides a critically important clarification of Who God is in our very troubled and confused times. And in it, Brague the Christian philosopher makes this observation about the God of Jesus Christ. And now I quote.

> *God does not seek our happiness. He does not seek our unhappiness. He seeks our good, which is to say, our sanctification. Our good, in other words, is God Himself.*

And all of this is about love because to love in the way that Jesus our Lord uses the word is to seek the good of the other, and the greatest good of anyone, the ultimate and final good, for which every person has been created from the first to the last, is God Himself, the Father, the Son, and the Holy Spirit.

To love another is to seek to bring the other into a relationship of faith with Jesus Christ so that through Christ the other can know the Father and live in communion with Him through the Son. It is in this way that we can love everyone and anyone. To love another is to seek the other's good.

Thus, I can love my enemies, even my enemies, not to mention those I don't like and wouldn't invite into my home. "Love your neighbor as yourself," says the Lord. (Lk 10:27) "Love your enemies and those who persecute you," says the Lord. (Mt 5:44) "Love one another as I have loved you," says the Lord. (Jn 13:34)

To love is to seek the good of the other. And it is necessary to understand this in order to understand the word of God for us today. "If you love me," says the Lord, "you will keep my commandments." (Jn 14:15) To love another person is to seek his good. But we cannot seek the Lord's good because He is goodness itself. Therefore the form of the love of God is to keep His commandments.

How can we know that Jesus loved God the Father? "I do as the Father has commanded me, so that the world may know that I love the Father." (Jn 14:31)

No goodness, no happiness.
No obedience, no love.

We know that God the Son loves His heavenly Father because He does what the Father commands Him to do. "I came," says the Lord, "not to do My Own will, but the will of Him Who sent Me." (Jn 6:38) And that's the only way the world will know that we love God.

Hear then the word of the Lord.

> If a man loves Me, he will keep My word, and My Father will love him and We will come to him and make Our home with him. He who does not love Me does not keep My words and the word which you hear is not Mine but the Father's Who sent Me. (Jn 14:23-24)

> If you keep My commandments, you will abide in My love just as I keep My Father's commandments and abide in His love. These things have I spoken to you that My joy may be in you and that your joy may be full. (Jn 15:10-11)

To love God is to keep His commandments. And when I keep His commandments — and only when I keep His commandments — do I love you as Jesus loves me.

Amen.

PART II

Simplicity

The Twist

The eternal perspective is a present reality but it's a very hard attitude to maintain, you know what I mean? I'll think about it in my prayers — I'll think... yes, that's right! — and then I just slip so easily back. Everything in this world is organized to draw me into that, right? Everything.

Did you read this book, *Thoughts Matter*? Sister Meg Funk. Do you know that book? I subscribed to this thing from Liturgical Press called This Day. It's a monthly thing, it's got all the readings and all this other stuff for mass for every day in the month, and stuff for morning prayer and evening prayer. Rufino introduced me to it, gave me a copy. And so I subscribed for a year or two. Every day there is a... If there's a saint's day there's something about the saint usually, like a biography or something. And then you'll find a little reflection by different people. And there's a thing there from Meg Funk, I'm sure it's gotta be the Meg Funk who did *Thoughts Matter*. And it's about the camel going through the eye of the needle. (Mt 19:24, Mk 10:25, Lk 18:25) And she says what if this is really and literally true? What does this mean? And then she says... It's very touching. I'm keeping it (the only thing I'm keeping from this month!) She said, I think it's like a promise, a great word. When I die, I won't be able to take any of this stuff, and I won't need any of this stuff. I won't need anything. And that's why I'll be able to get through this narrow way. I will be unencumbered because I can't take all my obligations, all my stuff, all my commitments. Everything. So I can enter into the joy of the Lord.

And I thought, that was really very moving to me. You know? I don't know how sound an interpretation of that verse it is, but it's good enough! Because I think it's the truth on a deeper level, you know? To die in Christ is finally to... It's not like you're going to lose everything. That was the twist. It's not like you're going to lose everything. Or that you have to give everything up. It's just that you're not going to need any of that stuff, whatever it is.

And I thought like, yeah that's right. And so how much of that stuff do I need now? You know? What do I need now? If I don't need it then, do I really...

Now I know I have needs. But I mean, what am I encumbering myself with unnecessarily?

5

So Complicated!

*In the name of the Father and of the Son
and of the Holy Spirit.*

Watch and pray at all times, praying that you may have
strength to escape all these things that will take place,
and to stand before the Son of man.

Lk 21:36

As I just mentioned to the children, this is the beginning
of a new church year, a new liturgical year which is all built
around the reading of the gospel according to St. Luke.
Many of us have a particular love of Advent, its customs,
its music, its ceremonies and symbols. And the preemi-
nent symbol, liturgical symbol at least, of Advent is the
advent wreath. The advent wreath is of Lutheran origin
and has spread to I think every nook and cranny of the
universal church. You can find advent wreaths everywhere

these days. And in my childhood memory of the advent wreath, there was a wreath with four white candles and, as you know, each Sunday one is lit until they are all lit on the fourth Sunday of Advent, and then the wreath gives way to the Christmas tree filled with light and symbolizing the coming of the true light that enlightens every man, the light of the world, Jesus Christ.

Simple things, however, can become... complicated. And they usually do! Somewhere along the line, the candles became purple. Well, almost purple. One of them is not purple; one of them is pink, or rose. And when that happened, one of the questions I've been asked repeatedly for the last thirty or forty years is, "What's with that pink candle anyway? What's that about?" "When is it lit, and why isn't it the same color as all the others?" This has become to me what I call the Great Advent Mystery.

Here I should mention (then again, I probably shouldn't), that there's also a custom of red advent candles but why complicate matters even more than they already are? As for the rose or pink candle, it's lit on the third Sunday of Advent, which is called Rejoice Sunday after the Latin introit for the day, and was meant to relieve the penitential atmosphere of the season. Purple, you see, is the color of penance in christian symbolism, and Advent was for centuries understood to be a little Lent, a season of fasting and prayer and preparation for the celebration of the birth of the Savior just as Lent prepares us similarly through fasting and prayer for the celebration of the Lord's death and resurrection.

Well, penance fell out of favor quite some time ago. I suspect that it was maybe in the 1960s. Maybe it was in 1967. For those of you who are under fifty, that was the "summer of love." In any event, who wants to think of their sins anyway? Right? Especially during this happy time when every store is playing Rudolph the Red-nosed Reindeer! And so the color of Advent changed to blue. (Unless, of course, you're in the chapel where it's still purple!*) So you can take your pick, you know, whether you want to have a happier blue Advent or a penitential purple Advent. And then of course, blue is chosen because it's the color of the Blessed Virgin Mary; it's the color of hope. And that raises the question finally of, what do we do about that pink candle? Since Advent is no longer a penitential season, do we still need the pink candle? Why can't we just have all blue candles? Well, that's a good question. An imponderable question that I'm not prepared to answer.

Well, that's how simple things become complicated.

The whole pattern of the Biblical narrative is one of promise and fulfillment. And the first Sunday of Advent is an annual occasion to remember our Lord's promise to come

---

* St. Michael's still has on its property the original church and has services there with older vestments and traditions.

51

again in glory to judge the living and the dead, and to bring all things to fulfillment in God. The truth is that that's a promise that's easy to forget. After all, it's been two thousand years (right?) since our Lord made that promise, and there are so many other things to think about, for instance, like the color of the candles on the advent wreath.

And it's about that very thing that our Lord warns us in today's gospel.

> Heaven and earth will pass away but my words will not pass away. But take heed to yourselves lest your hearts be weighed down in dissipation and drunkenness and cares of this life, and that day come upon you suddenly like a snare, for it will come upon all who dwell on the face of the whole earth. (Lk 21:33-35)

In a world heedless of the living God and as indifferent to His promises as it is hostile to His commandments, our greatest threat may be what the Lord calls the cares of this life. And in truth, while the world may be fleeing from God, it nevertheless demands that we care. Care, that is, about the things that the world cares about. The cares of this life multiply extravagantly. It seems that as soon as one problem is solved or one anxiety overcome, two, four, or six others rise up to take its place. And without doubt these cares do take us away from God, they dull our memory of both His commandments and His promises, and lead us into the realm of forgetfulness.

It's this forgetfulness that the Lord is cautioning us against. The remedy He tells us is to watch and pray. By watchfulness and prayer we will overcome the distracting presence of our inevitable cares. We can watch and pray anywhere and everywhere, even while shopping for those Christmas presents. And maybe that's the best time and place to watch and to pray. All that's required of us is the remembrance of God and His promises.

And so the colors of the advent season may change and evolve, but they're all appropriate. Advent is a time for repentance, that is, a time to turn away from sin and turn to the living God. So purple is right. And it's a time to rejoice because God has promised us the kingdom. And so rose is good. And it's a time to hope because when we stand before the Lord on the last day, we will not stand before Him as strangers but as His Own adopted brothers and sisters. And so blue, the color of hope, is good.

The first Christians believed that the best thing that will ever happen to this world will be the coming of the Lord in glory. They expected it to happen any day, and they prayed for it continuously. May our Lord grant us the grace to watch and to pray for His appearing.

Amen.

6

What Is Enough?

In the name of the Father, and of the Son,
and of the Holy Spirit.

In 1965, the year I completed my university education, Mick Jagger and the Rolling Stones recorded "Satisfaction." As in, "I can't get no satisfaction." Yes, Mick sang, "I can't get no satisfaction 'cause I try and I try and I try and I try...

> *I can't get no satisfaction,*
> *no no no no satisfaction.*

That, from the land of Shakespeare. I leave you to ponder that. Those Brits have such a way with language, you know? Well, this immortal poetry has stuck with me since then because I thought then and I think now if a bunch of spoiled, over-indulged fabulously wealthy rock stars can't get no satisfaction, who can?

Well, the word 'satisfaction' comes directly from the Latin, from the word satis, which translates into English as 'enough' or 'sufficient.' The question is, can anything satisfy us? Can we ever have enough? Can we ever enjoy sufficiency? The great Spanish mystic, Teresa of Ávila, said (and it does pain me to quote her after quoting Mick Jagger and Keith Richards, you know? In any event, she said,) "Everything is nothing." By which I take her to mean that everything is insufficient. Hence, poor Mick's lament.

What I have to say now I have to preface with a disclaimer. I am making no political statement of any kind; I have been convinced for decades that using the pulpit to promote any political agenda whatsoever is an abuse both of the preaching office and of you, the faithful. But having said that, I do want to speak to you of what we all know and cannot escape hearing about except by employing the most extraordinary means: the national and state economies. How did the richest, most innovative, enterprising, and prosperous nation in the entire history of the world end up massively in debt and debt beyond imagining? How did California, the Golden State, end up with the second highest unemployment rate in the nation, higher than Michigan, or West Virginia, or forty-five and more other states? I'm not pointing fingers— I'm not a politician nor an economist. I possess opinions (which I will not share,) but I possess no expertise. I'm concerned with these questions because of the underlying spiritual issues that are involved.

Why would a nation and a state rich beyond all known standards anywhere ever, economic magnets drawing people from all over the world, need to borrow to the point of bankruptcy? Friday I heard that the Apple Corporation has greater cash reserves than the Treasury of the United States. That's something to think about. (Probably better to think about Mick Jagger!)

Thirty years ago I was informed by people who were supposed to know, that California had the fifth largest economy in the whole world. There were only four nations in the world with a greater economy than California's, and one of them was the United States. Recently I read that after all that's befallen us, we still have the seventh largest economy in the world and yet, year after year after year, we have a budget crisis: the state cannot make ends meet.

I'm persuaded that at the heart of the problem, there is a fact that's denied and ignored and it's not a political or economic fact, it's that we human beings can never have enough. No matter how much we have, we just can't get no satisfaction. And our response to this problem, from the beginning of time, is always the same. What we need is... More. If we just have more, we'll at last have enough. And from the beginning of time, the good God Who made us has tried to disabuse us of this fallacy.

Consider the story of our first parents in the garden of

Eden at the very beginning of the Bible. The Lord God gives them... everything. Except the fruit of one tree. Everything else is theirs to eat. But it wasn't enough.

The Lord gave Israel bread in the wilderness. But they cried out, "He brought us out here to die, and we have nothing to eat but this worthless manna." It wasn't enough.

The Lord God gave Israel the land flowing with milk and honey, but it wasn't enough.

The Lord gave David His chosen, everything. Except Bathsheba. It wasn't enough.

Listen to the Lord's lament over David His chosen one, delivered through the prophet Nathan.

> I anointed you King over Israel, and I delivered you out of the hand of Saul. And I gave you your master's house, and your master's wives, into your bosom. And gave you the House of Israel and of Judah. And if this were too little, I would add to you as much more. Why have you despised the word of the Lord to do what is evil in His sight? (2Sam 12:7-9)

As you know, David's evil began with coveting. And then idolatry. And then adultery. And then moved through lying, cheating, conspiring against the innocent, climaxed in murder. I leave it to you to add up how many of the ten commandments he managed to break. All because he just didn't have enough. He just couldn't get no satisfaction, hm? Remember, he stole Bathsheba even though he possessed a large harem of wives and concubines. David replicated the sin of Adam.

Today's Gospel is about human scarcity and God's abundance. Israel is once again in the wilderness, a lonely place apart. And Israel is hungry. But there's not enough to feed such a large multitude. The disciples tell the Lord, "We have only five loaves here, and two fish." The Lord tells them, "Bring them here to Me."

> Then He ordered the crowds to sit down on the grass. And taking the five loaves and two fish, He looked up to heaven, and blessed, and broke, and gave the loaves to the disciples, and the disciples gave them to the crowds. And they all ate and were satisfied. (Mt 14:19-20)

And to emphasize the point, we hear that they took up twelve baskets full of the broken pieces left over. There is a most important parallel here with the wedding at Cana, when the wedding guests ran out of wine and the Lord provided, not just more wine, but an ocean of the best wine, more wine than they could possibly consume.

God made man, male and female, a hungry being, an embodied soul who must eat in order to live. For man, the spiritual and the material are inseparable, for man is an embodied soul and for man, food is always much, much more than nutrition. It symbolizes both our material and spiritual need. Nothing so distinguishes man from the animals than our relationship with food. And that's why the Bible is about food and about eating from the very beginning until the very end and everywhere in between.

Consider the first reading for today from Isaiah. (Is 55:1-5) Consider the psalm we just recited together. (Ps 145:8-9,15-22) And I could enumerate so many passages we'd still be here next Sunday... so I won't do it.

Notice how our Lord's words and deeds in the wilderness foreshadow the words of institution of the Holy Eucharist.

> In the night in which He was betrayed, our Lord Jesus
> Christ took bread. And when He had given thanks,
> (that is, looked up to heaven) He brake it, and gave it
> to His disciples,

who have in turn given it to us.

The Church is the New Israel, wandering through the wilderness of this world to our true home. And we are still fed by the Lord with miraculous food. In the words of the Letter to the Hebrews, "Here we have no lasting city but we seek the city which is to come." (Heb 13:14) And because this is so, St. Peter refers to us as "exiles and aliens." (1Pet 2:11)

After His baptism, our Lord—Who would create the New Israel, Who was the New Israel in embryo—was Himself driven by the Spirit into the wilderness. And there He fasted and was tempted by the devil to satisfy His hunger by turning stones into bread. Our Lord responded by quoting the fifth book of Moses, the book of Deuteronomy, (Dt 8:3)

> Man shall not live by bread alone but by every word
> that proceeds from the mouth of God.

Man lives by bread but not by bread alone. "But by every word that proceeds from the mouth of God."

Today, right now, we are here to receive miraculous food from the hand of the Lord. We're here to receive the body of Christ which is the bread of heaven. And it is the bread which nourishes because our Lord Jesus Christ is the definitive and final word proceeding from the mouth of God and therefore the word of God and the bread of God have become one, and the Lord gives it to us in order to give us Himself.

Man lives by bread but not by bread alone.

We can find satisfaction—and I hope we do, in the things of this world, in all the good things of this world that God has created for us—when we understand that nothing in this world can ever satisfy us. Without God and apart from God, everything is nothing. The answer to our insatiable hunger is not More but God. Only our Lord Himself is enough. "They all ate and were satisfied."

I began by quoting Mick Jagger, and in an act of penance I shall close by quoting again St. Teresa of Ávila.

> Let nothing disturb you. Let nothing frighten you. All things pass away. God never changes. Patience obtains all things. He who has God, finds that he lacks nothing. God alone suffices.

Amen.

7

On a Journey

In the name of the One True God:
the Father, the Son, and the Holy Spirit.

At the end of the third and the beginning of the fourth century of the Christian era, Christian men began to go out into the deserts of Egypt, Syria, and Palestine to lead lives of solitude and prayer. The great majority of them were laymen, and this was a spontaneous movement; truly it was a movement of the Spirit. And the men who went there became revered and were given the title, "Abba," or Father. Today they are known collectively as the Desert Fathers. All that we have come to know as Christian monasticism grows from their words and their example, as does most Christian contemplative and ascetic life in — or out — of monasteries.

One of these figures from the desert of the fourth century, was Serapion the Sidonite, and one of the stories told about him goes like this.

> Abba Serapion travelled once on pilgrimage to Rome. There he was told of a celebrated recluse, a woman who lived always in one small room praying, and never going out. Sceptical about her way of life, for he himself was a great wanderer, Serapion called on her and asked, Why are you sitting here? To which she replied, I'm not sitting; I'm on a journey.

So she was, and so are you, and so am I. To believe and to be baptized means to be addressed by our Lord, and the primal imperative our Lord addresses to each one of us is, "Follow Me." We Christians are, first and foremost, followers.

Now when anyone says, "Follow me," I have to ask where he's going, where the person wants to lead me. The Lord has made it abundantly clear that He is leading those who follow Him through this world to the land of the Just, to His Father's house, to the heavenly Jerusalem, to the Kingdom of God. Our Lord said, "I am the Way, the Truth, and the Life; no one comes to the Father except by Me." And in the beginning our faith was not known as "Christianity," but it was known simply as "The Way." This led Dorothy Day to declare, "All the way to Heaven is Heaven because Jesus is the Way."

Our Lord Jesus Christ knows the way to the Father because He has come from the Father. He knows the way and He is the Way, and this Way is truly the Way of Life.

The Lord prayed that we would be in the world but not of the world because this world is passing away and we are passing through. All the readings appointed for this Sunday call us to remember that we are on a journey from this world to the Kingdom, that all journeys are filled with perils.

The reading from Genesis tells us that Abraham, who had left everything, his home, his family, all that he knew, to follow the Lord Who had promised Him numberless descendants, ended up many years later in a strange land, childless, and he was filled with anxiety because it seemed that his life was going nowhere. And he cried out to the Lord in that anxiety and this morning we heard the Lord's response to him. "Fear not, Abram, I am your shield; your reward shall be very great." (Gen 15:1) But as we know, Abraham didn't live to see that reward.

The Letter to the Hebrews acknowledges this. And so we heard in the second reading from the Letter to the Hebrews that

> The patriarchs of Israel all died in faith not having received what was promised. They were strangers and exiles on the earth; they were seeking a homeland, they desired a better country, that is, a heavenly one.

> Therefore, God is not ashamed to be called their God,
> for He has prepared for them a city. (Heb 11:13-16)

And the Letter to the Hebrews, goes on to tell us that if we follow the Lord Jesus Christ, we also are to "seek the city which is to come." (Heb 13:14)

For this reason, St. Peter in his first letter describes us in the same way that Paul described the patriarchs of Israel. He calls us "strangers and exiles in this world." (1Pet 2:11)

In the Gospel, our Lord tells us to sell our possessions, give alms, provide ourselves with purses that do not grow old with a treasure in the heavens that does not fail, where no thief approaches and no moth destroys. "For where our treasure is," He tells us, "there will be our heart also." (Mt 6:21, Lk 12:34) He is not urging us to embrace material destitution, but to be detached from all earthly treasures for they will all pass away like the earth itself. Only God and His Kingdom are forever. This world is full of wonders; we live in one of the most beautiful places on the face of the earth, it's filled with great beauty, and in it we receive the primal blessing of the Lord — Life — and all His other blessings. And we should rejoice in them and they should inspire in us gratitude.

Gratitude, you know, really is the sign of a healthy person. And we are here this morning to offer Eucharist, that is, thanksgiving, the fundamental act of Christian worship and adoration.

ॐ

But this is also a fallen world filled with great evil and many perils. It's truly a haunt of devils. Recall if you will, that our Lord called the devil the prince of this world. And while denying the existence of the prince, the media reports daily the effects of his presence everywhere and exhorts us to be afraid. That's really the message that comes through the newspapers, the radio, the television, and every other outlet every day. Be afraid. High anxiety, as I like to call it, is the order of the day, every day.

The war. Global warming. Second-hand smoke. (I really do love pointing out to people that I quit smoking twenty-two years ago and I thought I was safe, you know, I thought I had made it — and now I have to fear everybody else's smoke. There's always something to fear, you know? That's the way it runs.) The depletion of the rain forest. Toys from China (not to mention the food). Cholesterol (we're all terrorized by cholesterol — all the males out there, like me, are probably taking that expensive medication, right?) Nile virus. Chaos in the financial markets. And then of course there are the Muslim fanatics, crazies strapping dynamite on themselves, ready to appear at our airport at any time, and appearing at other airports around the world. That's a short list. I'm sure you could add ten or fifteen or twenty more items. That's the short list of all of what I call the Threats and the Frets, real and imagined, possible and probable, that haunt us currently. Right?

But I'm not too impressed really, because when I was in the sixth grade, the Willoughby-Eastlake School District, where I was a student, issued me and every other student in the school system a dog tag. And we got that dog tag so that when that inevitable nuclear war between us and the Soviet Union erupted, our remains could be identified, should there be any remains remaining. (I wasn't so sure.)

Along with the inevitable nuclear war with the Soviets (who remembers them now?) I also remember the coming ice age, and I believe I'm one of the only people who does. I thought that San Diego would become another Nome. (This was in the seventies, you know.) We were all going to freeze to death. But now I have hope... of beachfront property! It's a better outcome, isn't it? Well, unless you live on the beach. One more thing to worry about!

Do you remember the depletion of the ozone? We were all going to die, all of us, from terrible skin cancers; when the ozone layer disappeared, we would all perish. Somebody going out the door after the last mass said to me, "Remember radon?" I hadn't, but it's a good one to recall. Radon.

The population bomb, followed by mass famine and starvation; the whole world would die of hunger. And then, if this weren't enough, in the good old days, my father was always reminding me that smoking would stunt my growth. There's always something to worry about, isn't there?

Now, these things are real. And the evils in the world

are real and some are more threatening than others, and some of us take some of them more seriously than others, but the fact is that what you will never read in the newspapers, hear on the radio or on the television or anywhere else except a place like this, is that these things cannot imperil us on our journey. None of these things can keep us from reaching our destination. To paraphrase St. Paul, (Rom 8:38-39) "Neither global temperature change (up or down), Muslim fanatics, nor cholesterol can separate us from the love of God in Christ Jesus." Hmm? So none of these things actually can be absolutized because, no matter what, they will not keep us, the Lord tells us, from reaching our destination.

But there is something that can, and will, which you will never hear about anywhere else, and that's sin. Sin can separate us from the Lord, and He is the only One Who knows the way because He is the Way and if we become separated from Him, and only sin can separate us from Him, then we become really and truly lost. Lost souls.

To the sojourner Abram, the Lord said, "Fear not; I am your shield." And we do need a shield. "Your reward will be very great." (Gen 15:1) And to us the Lord says, "Fear not, little flock, for it is your Father's good pleasure to give you the Kingdom." (Lk 12:32) We are to enjoy the good things of this world, and this life, to rejoice in them and to be grateful

68

for them, but we are cautioned not to cling to them, not to absolutize them, because they will pass away. And we are to view the evils with realism, but without undue anxiety, because they will pass away, too. And we are passing through, on our way to our home.

We will reach our destination, the imperishable city our Lord has prepared for those who love Him, if we continue to follow the One Who knows the way. Whether we're world travelers like Serapion the Sidonite, or live our entire lives in the same house on the same street like the anchoress in Rome, we are on a journey home. And in just a few minutes, we will receive from the Lord Himself become our bread, to nourish us and to sustain us on the way. Don't be afraid.

Amen.

8

Nice v. Good

*In the name of the Father and of the Son
and of the Holy Spirit.*

A long time ago in another life I was teaching in a music studio in the north side of Pittsburgh. And on Saturdays I would cross the street to the Rosa Villa Cafe, a local bar and grill. And over time I noticed in a booth in the back facing the door was a white-haired gentleman who always wore black slacks and white dress shirt open at the neck, and there would be a parade of people coming in and they would go to his table and stand there and talk to him and sometimes families would come in. They would come in with their wives and children and they would stand there and talk to the man in the back. And I was busy thinking about the Debussy Rhapsody for clarinet so I wasn't paying a lot of attention.

But one Saturday as I was eating my grilled cheese,

two instrument salesmen that I had known and worked with for a long time, Benny Bongiovanni and Ross Prestia, came in and they sat down with me and we were eating and one of them said, "Do you know who that is in the back booth?" And I said, no, I have no idea who that is. And they said, "That's Big John LaRocca, the mafia don." Big John, who also owned a cement factory. That's true! He owned the Rosa Villa and he held court there all the time and people would come in to see him.

So after that I, you know, tried to be inconspicuous about it but, I would kinda keep an eye on things as I was eating. And I'd notice that he was always, as I had actually noticed before, gracious and very nice to the wives and children. Very courteous, you know.

Now the reason I tell this story is because it illustrates a great truth. And that is that the nice are not always good, and the good are not always nice. Being nice and being good are not synonyms.

Our Lord Jesus Christ is always good. He is the summation of all goodness but he's not always nice. You'll know that if you read the gospels. St. Paul certainly is not always nice, as you will know if you read the epistles of St. Paul. Niceness is a matter of social convention, that which we accept as nice is that which we agree on among ourselves. We determine who and what is nice and what's not. But goodness is revealed to us by God Who is Himself alone good.

The cultural crisis of our time is in large part the result of the embrace of the nice as defined by us and the rejection of the good as defined by God.

Our Lord made it abundantly clear that He was the One sent by the Lord God to Israel. He was the anointed one of God, the Messiah promised to Israel and that He came above all to call the Jews back to their Lord and God. A gentile had no part in the covenant community and had no claim on Him. Hence His response to the Syrophoenician woman, the gentile, in today's gospel.

Now I don't know if His response bothers you but it bothered me for a very long time. It really did. Here's a woman whose daughter is possessed and she pleads with the Lord to cast out the demon. And how did our Lord respond to this poor woman in distress?

> Let the children (that is, the Israelites) be fed first, for
> it's not right to take the children's bread and throw it
> to the (gentile) dogs. (Mk 7:27)

That's what our Lord said to her. Now I ask you, is that nice? No! It's not nice.

For a long time I set myself up as judge over God, which is an easy thing to do. Right? I considered myself so much more courteous, polite, thoughtful, kind — you know — than Him. I imagined I would have said to this poor woman in distress,

> *I'm so sorry! You're a gentile. (Not that there's anything wrong with that!) But first I have to take care of the Israelites. Don't misunderstand! You're just as good as they are and I love you just as much, but I can't take care of you today and I hope you'll understand.*

Now, wouldn't that have been nicer, kinder and gentler? Of course, but it wouldn't have been true, would it? It would not have expressed the truth that our Lord expressed when He responded to the woman.

When the Samaritan woman at the well talked to our Lord, she asked our Lord, "Where's the right place to worship, Jerusalem or Mount Gerazim? Jerusalem where the Jews worship, or on this holy mount, Gerazim, where my people the Samaritans worship?" The Lord did not equivocate. He did not say to her, "Oh, all religions are just paths to the same place and I'm sure you're sincere in your beliefs." You know? "Don't worry about it!" No. He didn't say that. He said to her, (Jn 4:22)

> You worship what you do not know. We Israelites worship what we know, for salvation is from the Jews.

The truth is that different religions are different paths to very different destinations, and our Lord was clear about

73

that even if people do not want to hear that word. It is the truth that our Lord placed before the Samaritan woman just as He placed truth before the Syrophoenician woman, as He places the truth before all of us. And as Flannery O'Connor (one of my favorite people in literature) put it, "The truth doesn't change according to our ability to stomach it." Our Lord is the Way, the Truth, and the Life. He is the Truth incarnate.

But if we leave things here, I believe that we will have missed the point of the story. Although the woman was a gentile, she called Jesus "Lord." And she had faith in His power to heal her daughter. She didn't become indignant at the Lord for His insult, but acknowledged the truth of what He said. And she responded by saying, in acknowledging that truth, "Yes Lord, yet even the dogs under the table eat the children's bread that falls from it."

We should know that she acknowledged Jesus as Lord and she placed the welfare of her stricken daughter before herself and her own dignity. Only the humble can have faith and she is above all, humble. St. Matthew tells us that the Lord said to her,

> O woman, great is your faith; be it done for you as you desire. (Mt 15:28)

The woman was not an Israelite; she was not part of the covenant community and she had no claim on Jesus. Yet she adhered to Him by faith, and it was to her faith that the Lord responded, as He does to our faith.

But if the first healing story is about humility and faith, the second is about pride and unbelief.

A deaf mute was brought to the Lord and He was asked to lay His hand upon him. The Lord clearly did not want to make a public spectacle of this matter and dealt with the man in private. The man's tongue was released and he spoke plainly. And the Lord charged the man and his friends to "tell no one."

> But the more He charged them, the more zealously they proclaimed it. (Mk 7:36)

Only the humble can obey. Those who brought our Lord the deaf-mute wanted Him to heal the man but they did not want to use their faculty of hearing to listen to Him. As for the power of speech, He charged them to tell no one and the more He charged them, the more they used the faculty of speech to disobey Him. They wanted the gift, the healing, but they did not want the giver, they did not want a Lord and God. They had ears but they would not listen, and they could speak but the things they said should have remained unspoken. Paradoxically, while they believed He had the power to heal, they had no faith in Him. They praised His power but would not honor Him as their Lord.

Of course, we can agree that their astonishment was appropriate and their public praises of the Lord were justified, but by doing so we would place ourselves among the proud who know better than the Lord what's right and what's good.

Those in the second story are vivid contrasts to the gentile woman in the first story. She listened to the Lord. And having listened, responded to what He said rather than to what she — or we — might have wished He had said. She did not contend with Him, but received His words with humility, accepted them, and responded to Him with trust. And she was rewarded.

In all this, our Lord Himself is the model, the exemplar, for He said over and over again, "I came not to do my own will but the will of Him Who sent Me." (Jn 6:38) And while He prayed in the garden that the cross might be taken from Him, nevertheless He humbled Himself and became obedient unto death, even death on a cross.

We who are the children of God, are called to use the faculty of hearing to listen to Him even when His words are disturbing or distasteful or disagreeable to us. And we are to use the faculty of speech to praise Him as He wills to be praised and not as we will to praise Him.

Amen.

PART III

Faith

The Liberation of Fr. Ivor

I've spent this year, basically trying to be retired, trying to actually be done. You know, retired, and all that
that means. And one of the things I've been doing is,
I've started to read the Bible. *Really, Father?* Yeah, I've
started to read the Bible now. I used to… I was never
ever able to read… almost any serious literature without thinking about classes, sermons, how was I going to
convey this, how do I explain this, what does this really
mean, I have to figure these out, someone's going to ask
me, Father, what does this mean? Pastor, what does that
mean? I mean, it's my job and I gotta have an answer. I
don't want to always be saying, Gosh, you got me!

So now, I'm actually for the first time reading scripture
without any of that. And it's a whole different experience.
A whole different experience to read it, to try and listen
to the Lord speaking to me without that thing always,
like what do I have to make of this, how can I explain
this. I don't know if I'm making any sense, but just kind
of openness to it, the word of God. Without attending to
how this comes up in the lectionary and this is relevant

to that, and I can see the connection to this, and I have to teach that class on whatever. You know what I mean? You just keep going and churning, churning, churning and never letting go.

Of course, before I went to seminary, I used to read the Bible kind of the way I'm reading it now. But of course, I didn't know the things I know now. When you go to seminary, you're there to learn. Then you get into the thing of well, I have to figure this out. I need to understand this. Now, I'm glad I did it, although forty-five years of doing that makes me able to read it now in a different way. You know what I mean? It's the Lord speaking to me and me trying to listen to the Lord without all that stuff going on. It's very freeing. I hate to say it, but it's liberating.

9

Gypsies and Heretics

In the name of the Father, and of the Son,
and of the Holy Spirit.

My father was the second-born of my grandparents' seven children. When I was born, the second grandchild of my grandparents and the first grandson, my father's family all lived within walking distance of one another. I lived in the constant presence of my large family, and although my mother worked, I never knew what a babysitter was.

My father was in the building trades, and after the war (that's World War II), Cleveland was a boom town, and we did the unthinkable—we moved. My grandmother, the matriarch, was not pleased, and began to call us… the gypsies. Hm? That amused me then, and it still amuses me. Although we lived in another city, we went home constantly to Pittsburgh for Christmas and Easter, Fourth of July, Memorial Day, anniversaries, and birthdays. Lots of birthdays. We were always assembling to celebrate someone or something. I lived in a world of grandparents, aunts, uncles, and cousins.

When I was in my early twenties, my grandmother died, and the family was never together again. Not once. I had always been aware of just how different my father and his siblings were. (Today, we would call them a diverse group of people, no doubt.) What I had never grasped was that they were united by their mother, and when she was gone, there was no one to bring them together.

Today is Ascension Sunday, and the account of this very mysterious and important event is found in today's first reading from the Acts of the Apostles. (Acts 1:6-14) Our Lord Jesus Christ appeared to His disciples and apostles for several weeks after His resurrection. He spoke with them, He ate with them, He invited them to touch Him and to see that He was not a ghost but had flesh and bone. And St. Paul tells us that He appeared at one point to more than five hundred people at one time. But after these many appearances, He was—as we just heard—lifted up and a cloud took Him out of their sight.

This cloud is the cloud of the divine presence, the shekinah, sometimes referred to as the glory of the Lord. Jesus had returned to the One He called His God and our God, His Father and our Father. In the words of Leo the

Great, our Lord's visible presence has passed into the sacraments, which are animated by the Holy Spirit which He promised to send us.

One of the most interesting parts of the Ascension narrative found in Acts, at least one of the most interesting parts of it to me, is easy to overlook.

> So when the apostles had come together, they asked Jesus, Lord, will you at this time restore the kingdom to Israel? (Acts 1:6)

What they mean by that is,

> *Well now are You finally going to declare Yourself to be the ultimate and final David, get together a big army, defeat the Romans, and make Jerusalem the navel of the universe?*

In other words, they still didn't get it despite everything that the Lord had said and all that He had done. That's astonishing and it's a reminder of how many times we have to hear things and experience them before we really grasp them.

Once more and for the last time, the Lord corrected them and promised them the power of the Holy Spirit so that they could be His witnesses in Jerusalem and all Judea and Samaria, and to the ends of the earth. And He gives us the Holy Spirit for exactly the same reason, so that we can be His witnesses everywhere and anywhere.

As for our Lord Himself, we should note that He ascended to the Father, incarnate—that is, with His crucified and resurrected body. Just as our Lord did not leave His body in the tomb and rise spiritually from the dead—that is, as a disembodied spirit or ghost, something that He actively wanted to impress on the apostles and disciples as He appeared to them—so He did not leave His body behind and ascend to the Father as a disembodied spirit, but ascended as He had been raised: bodily. Jesus is eternally true man, as well as true God, eternally embodied. In the person of Jesus, the Word of God made flesh, God has humanized Himself, and by ascending in the flesh, our Lord has made a place in God the Most Holy Trinity for us, His adopted brothers and sisters. Human beings are embodied souls, and our destiny is not to become angels—that is, disembodied spirits—but to become the men and women that God has created us to be.

As for our Lord Himself, it's worth asking what He's been doing since His ascension. This isn't an idle question of the sort that a student supposedly asked St. Augustine of Hippo. According to the story, which some of you may have heard me tell (more than once!) 'cause I always like to tell it when people ask me questions I don't want to answer, the great Augustine was asked what God was doing before He created the world. And the saint reportedly answered, "He was out in the woods cutting switches to beat people with who asked that question." You know, I don't even know if that's a true story but it's so good, it's such a good story. The question of our Lord's activity since His ascension, however, is of another sort. And the author of the Letter to the Hebrews gives us an answer.

Our Lord, He tells us, always lives to make intercession for us. (Heb 7:25) As to the content of that intercession of our Lord, we should look to today's Gospel, our Lord's intercessory prayer to the Father for us before His arrest and crucifixion.

I'm certain that most of us have heard that we are to be in the world but not of the world, but those words are not found in the Bible. That phrase is drawn, however, from our Lord's prayer reported by St. John, part of which we heard today. "I am praying for them. I am not praying for the world."

That's something to ponder.

> I am praying for them. I am not praying for the world, but for those whom You have given Me for they are yours. All mine are yours, and yours are mine, and I am glorified in them. (Jn 17:9-10)

Now you have to think about that. Ponder it. The Lord is telling the Father that He is glorified in us. That should cause you a little loss of sleep, hm? Or perhaps allow you to sleep more soundly! There's no reason whatsoever to believe that our Lord prayed this prayer two thousand years ago and then forgot about it. I believe that it is at the heart of His constant eternal intercession for us. The words our Lord spoke two thousand years ago He speaks to us today and the prayers He offered two thousand years ago He offers today.

> And now I am no more in the world but they are in
> the world. And I am coming to You. Holy Father, keep
> them in Your name which You have given Me that they
> may be one even as We are One. (Jn 17:11)

The 1960s were the decade of Christian unity. The World and National Council of Churches were in their heyday and the Roman Catholic Church held a great council, Vatican II, during which Rome began to make overtures to other Christians, and began to refer to us as "separated brethren."* We were all going to be one great happy family. Things turned out differently. The 1960s marked the beginning of a decline in church membership and church attendance unknown up until then. That decline has not yet ended, and Christians seem more divided than ever. If there is not greater division between denominations, there is far, far greater division

---

* At the 8am unrecorded but memorable service: "...instead of damned heretics."

within them. I'm convinced that the reason is that we became concerned with unity rather than with the Lord and the name revealed to us through Him. Indeed, the World Council of Churches and the National Council of Churches went so far as to declare that "doctrine divides, but service unites." But there is nothing that can unite the supernatural family of the Church other than our Lord Jesus Christ, its head and most important member.

And this brings me back to my father's family. They were united as a family as long as their attention was on my grandmother and not on one another. They were united by a person, and when she was gone, they ceased to assemble together and to celebrate together. They had never sought unity, they had sought the presence of the one who united them. To once again quote our Lord Jesus Christ, "let those who have ears to hear, hear."

Amen.

10

The Power to Explain Nothing

Sixteen years ago I returned home to find a message from my Aunt Myrtle. She sounded distressed and I returned her call immediately. The story she told was nothing less than incredible. Here I should explain that my "Aunt" Myrtle is the mother of a friend I met when we were both fifteen. My friend's father was an engineer and his mother a nurse who stayed home to raise their three sons, John, David and Daniel, each two years apart in age. And although I have a wonderful family, I loved them so much I wanted to be part of theirs too. We all grew up, married and had families. Daniel, his wife, son and daughter, moved to a small town. His son, an outstanding student, was class valedictorian; he was also popular and had many friends. His teachers loved

---

This sermon, not recorded, is Fr. Kraft's own typescript.

him and everyone predicted he would do great things. After graduation he left for one of the most prestigious universities in the country. Returning home for vacation after his freshman year, he got a summer job and then one night he entered his parents' bedroom with a knife and murdered his mother and attempted to murder his father. Thinking he was an intruder, his father fought with him but received a potentially fatal chest wound which punctured his lung. Unable to breathe, he fell to the kitchen floor incapable of further resistance. He was left there to die. The boy's sister, coming out of her room to see what was happening, returned to her room, locked the door and called the police. Her brother tried to get her to open the door and when she refused he went outside, broke in through a window and attacked her. She was strong and athletic and though she suffered many horrible defensive wounds, she managed to fend off her brother's relentless attack until the police arrived.

Understandably, my Aunt Myrtle was in shock. Speaking later to the boy's uncle I learned that he offered no explanation. As I remember, the family hired their own psychiatrist and psychologist, the best they could find, as did the state. No evidence of mental illness was detected by any of them. A plea bargain was struck, there was no trial and the matricide went to prison where he remains to this day.

As we all know, at a midnight showing of a movie, a local boy from Peñasquitos, twenty-four year old James Holmes murdered twelve people and wounded fifty-eight more. He also booby trapped his apartment. He grew up in a middle class, church going Lutheran family and was in Colorado working on a PhD in neuroscience. The chancellor of UC Riverside, referring to his academic achievements, called him "the top of the top."

The search for "reasons" is in full swing. I've noticed that in the first reports he was referred to as "quiet". Next he was described as a "loner". This morning the UT called him "odd". He used guns so, of course, guns are being blamed. Violent movies are also being blamed. At least one commentator has called him "deranged". This is something we'll no doubt hear often in coming days. "He must be crazy because only a crazy person would do such a thing." This is, of course, a fallacious argument.

The hallmark of our age is scientific rationality and the hallmark of scientific rationality is the ability to predict. Science looks for causes in order to predict and therefore control effects. Control is what it's all about and so we will once again be treated to an endless stream of "experts" explaining Holmes' behavior so as to prevent its recurrence. Their explanations will explain nothing; neither will they prevent anything.

Quantitatively, Holmes' crime was worse than the

crime of my Aunt Myrtle's grandson. Qualitatively it was not. To attempt to murder one's whole family is as terrible a crime as one can possibly commit. We'll hear much about the number of Holmes' victims as if it's about the numbers but I doubt that many people here or anywhere, know who Gary Ridgway is. Gary Ridgway is known in the annals of crime as The Green River Killer. He confessed to the murder of forty- eight women and very likely killed many more. He wasn't insane and he didn't use a gun.

There is something known in theology as the **mysterium iniquitatis**, a Latinism which translates, the mystery of evil. The "why" of what happened in Aurora Colorado is simpler and more mysterious than we want to admit. As I mentioned two weeks ago, God made us choosing beings. Every human being chooses, every day. You chose to get up this morning and come to this place. You could have chosen to do as numberless others have done. You could have chosen to sleep in, or you could have chosen to go to the beach, or chosen to sit in your favorite chair and read the paper. You did not. You chose to come here. Most choices are not that serious. They are so simple we fail to take proper note of them as conscious acts of will. Shall I have tacos for lunch today or enchiladas? (I've already decided to have Mexican food.)

Alexander Solzhenitsyn observed, "The line between

good and evil does not run between people but through every human heart." And so just as one chooses to get up for church or sleep in, or order tacos instead of enchiladas, everyone must choose between good and evil.

The God who made us, made us choosing beings and He will not take the power to choose from us. Faced with the most momentous choice we can make, the choice every one of us must make, the choice between good and evil, James Holmes, Gary Ridgway and my Aunt Myrtle's grandson chose evil and in so doing became the evil they chose. And because we don't want to believe that anyone would consciously choose evil we look for "reasons" but no reason will ever suffice. The human person, like the God who made us, is an unfathomable mystery, as is the choice to do evil and become the evil one chooses.

A relative of one of Holmes' murder victims has said, "I hope this evil act, that this evil man doesn't shake people's faith in God." I can't imagine why it should. Or perhaps I should say, I can't imagine why it should shake anyone's faith in the One True God, the Father, Son and Holy Spirit.

The living God is present in the world and this morning the Apostle Paul has forcibly reminded us that we who believe and are baptized are the locus of His Presence.

You and I, are the Temple of the Lord, "...in whom [we] also are built into it for **a dwelling place of God in the Spirit.**" (Eph 2:11-22) That's what the Church is, that's what you and I are, **the dwelling place of God in the Spirit.** The

Lord is present in you and in me and through us He calls to everyone He's made, inviting everyone to share in his life and love.

But to respond to Him means to choose the good, for as our Lord has told us, God alone is good. (Mk 10:18) Everyone has the power to turn to the God who has first turned to us, or to turn from him. To turn to him is to choose life and light. But we can also choose to turn from him into darkness and death.

How many would like this burden to be taken away from us, to believe that our lives and deeds are just the product of nurture or nature, that we choose nothing but are the product of forces beyond our control. But the truth is otherwise.

God the Father, Son and Holy Spirit is a communion of love and has created us to share in his love. **But only those who can choose, can love, which is why the living God will not take the power to choose from us.**

To live in this world is to live with the ever present choice between good and evil. And that means living not only with our own choices, but with the choices others make.

Therefore our Lord Jesus Christ has declared that his Kingdom *is not of this world*, and the Apostle reminds us that *here we have no lasting city but [must] seek the city which is to come.* And on the last day our Lord has promised to appear, not to justify His actions, but to judge ours.

11

Concealed and Revealed

In the name of the Father, and of the Son,
and of the Holy Spirit.

I suspect that many of us remember ABC's Wide World of Sports. It ran for a very long time: from 1961 to 1997. On Saturday afternoons, Jim McKay — the face and voice of Wide World of Sports — would intone the following words over a montage of sports clips. "Spanning the globe to bring you the constant variety of sport... the thrill of victory... and the agony of defeat... the human drama of athletic competition. This is ABC's Wide World of Sports."

I don't remember a single clip that showed the thrill of victory. But if you watched that show as I did, you will remember the agony of defeat. It was the crash, the terrible crash of a ski jumper named Vinko Bogataj, and it was awful, and that image is indelibly imprinted on my memory.

On this Sunday in the church year, we are all annually

tempted — perhaps by the Tempter himself — to turn what we've just seen and heard in the liturgy into an ecclesiastical or spiritual or theological Wide World of Sports. And it's a temptation which we have to resist. In the "Wide World of Sports" reading of Palm and Passion Sunday, we begin first with the thrill of victory.

Our Lord was welcomed not merely as a hero but as One Who came in the name of the Lord. The Lord had promised David, a thousand years before our Lord Jesus Christ came into the world, that he would be the first of an eternal dynasty. And that dynasty was lost when the Babylonians invaded Israel, destroyed the Temple, and carried off the Davidic descendant in 587 BC. "Blessed," proclaimed the crowd, "is the kingdom of our father David that is coming." (Mk 11:10) Our Lord was welcomed by Jerusalem as the final and victorious David. Observant Jews, I should add, are still awaiting such a figure to appear. And each year we Christians on this day commemorate the Lord's entry into Jerusalem remembering the cheering crowds with our procession and our palms.

Of course almost immediately things begin to fall apart. The bright picture of welcoming joy quickly turns dark and gets darker and darker and within days the crowd that had welcomed the Lord with such joy and enthusiasm, given the choice, prefer Barabbas the insurrectionist and murderer, and demand the Lord's crucifixion.

The conclusion of the story can be read as the story

of the agony of defeat. Right? In this telling of the story, the Lord dies rejected and abandoned by all, even by the God He called "My Father," crying out with His dying breath, "My God, my God, why hast Thou forsaken me?"

ABC's Wide World of Sports brought us the human drama of athletic competition. What I've just read could be called the human drama of the fallen hero Jesus. But if we hear the story of Palm Sunday and the Passion of our Lord in this way as simply a human drama, we will have missed everything. For hidden in the human drama is another drama, the divine drama, which the human drama both reveals and conceals.

Of course, what we've heard today is a human drama. It's the story of fallen humanity. Our Lord was surrounded by the depraved, the sadistic, the selfish, the godless, the fearful and the cowardly, the confused, the helpless and the hopeless, by those who mock God and, of course, those struggling always and forever for dominance and power. That's what it means, you know, to live in a fallen world. That's the world that we wake up to every day. And if you've somehow missed that, let me know! Because I want to know how you've avoided realizing that is the world in which we live, the world that has rejected its Creator and is at enmity with the God Who made it.

Our attention therefore is easily captured by the relationship our Lord has with those around Him, what I call the horizontal story. This is the story between our Lord and the people around Him. Jesus and the disciples who betray, desert, and deny Him. Jesus and the chief priest, elders, and scribes. Jesus and Pilate. Jesus and the crowd. Jesus and the soldiers who torment Him. Jesus and the passersby who mock Him. Jesus and the centurion. And you may have noticed that in St. Mark's telling, except for the laconic response that our Lord makes to Pilate, our Lord responds to none of these.

Beneath the human drama, there is the other drama that is both concealed and revealed. Concealed within the human drama, there is the divine drama. This is the vertical story. This is the mystery of the relationship between the Lord Jesus Christ and the God He calls "My Father." In His passion, the Lord does not speak to those around Him, He speaks to God. He made the words of the psalmist His Own. "My God, my God, why hast thou forsaken me?" are the first ten words of Psalm 22. The Lord has taken the psalm, like every faithful and pious Jew ever did for a thousand years, and He has made the psalm His Own prayer. And when we hear those words, we need to remember that they imply the entire psalm, and not just the first ten words. We should comprehend the entire psalm.

On Holy Thursday, during the stripping of the altar, we will recite all of Psalm 22. But today I want to read the final verses of that psalm which we cannot omit when we hear our Lord say, "My God, my God, why hast Thou for-saken me?" (Ps 22: 22-24, 29-31)

> I will tell of Thy name to my brethren,
>> in the midst of the congregation I will praise Thee.
> You who fear the Lord, praise Him.
>> All you sons of Jacob, glorify Him
>> and stand in awe of Him, all you sons of Israel.
> For He has not despised or abhorred
>> the affliction of the afflicted
> and He has not hid His face from him,
>> but has heard when he cried to Him.
>
> Yea, to Him shall all the proud of the earth bow down.
>> Before Him shall bow
>>> all who go down to the dust,
>> and he who cannot keep himself alive.
> Posterity shall serve Him.
>> Men shall tell of the Lord
>>> to the coming generations
> and proclaim His deliverance to a people yet unborn,
>> that He has wrought it.

And we are those people yet unborn at the time our Lord made this psalm His Own prayer from the cross.

This is what the Lord was praying in His final mo-ments. It's not a cry of dereliction but a prayer uttered to the

God and Father Who had sent Him into the world to bear the cross, to endure rejection, suffering, and crucifixion, to trust the Father Who promised to raise Him up from the dead on the third day and glorify Him.

What is revealed through the passion of our Lord is the mystery of the Triune God. The mystery of the loving Father Who eternally begets His Son and the eternal Son Who, in love, eternally offers Himself back to the Father. And this mystery becomes manifest in time and space in the passion of our Lord.

I believe it was Gregory Dix, the great Anglican theologian, who observed therefore that the passion of our Lord is the eternal transfixed in time. It is because of this mystery of the giving and self-giving of God in Himself, Who God is, that enables St. John the Apostle to say that God is Love. But to hear the divine drama concealed in the human drama, we do not need to turn to anyone other than the apostle Paul who tells the story of the Lord's life, death, and sufferings with virtually no reference to the human drama. He tells it as pure vertical story.

> Have this mind among yourselves which you have in Christ Jesus Who, though He was in the form of God, did not deem equality with God something to be grasped, but emptied Himself, taking the form of a

servant, and being found in human form He humbled
Himself and became obedient unto death, even death
on a cross. Therefore, God has highly exalted Him.

And you will notice that there are no disciples, centurions, sadistic soldiers, crazed priests, or anybody else in that story. That is the divine drama revealed and concealed in the human drama.

The Lord's victory on this day is not His entrance into Jerusalem when a fickle crowd, so easily turned into a rabid mob, welcomed Him. Our Lord's victory came when He mounted the cross in humility and loving trust for the Father in the conviction that the Father had sent Him to offer Himself on the cross. He did this in loving trust and trusting love. And when He breathed His last, He became victorious. It is a story of victory but not the apparent one.

The victory, the victory is completed when the Lord offers Himself to the Father in obedient, loving trust. And when He offers Himself, He becomes victor, victor over the enemy, the enemy of God and man, the prince of darkness, the father of lies, and all those who are seduced by him.

Amen.

12

Getting the Picture

*In the name of the Father, and of the Son,
and of the Holy Spirit.*

The Lord is my shepherd;
    I shall not want,
He maketh me to lie down in green pastures.

Ps 23:1-2

I'm certain we're all familiar with the Chinese proverb, "One picture is worth a thousand words." Of course, there are different kinds of pictures. There are those pictures we see with our eyes and those we see with the imagination. Today is Good Shepherd Sunday and it evokes images just as our Lord intended when He declared Himself to be the good shepherd.

Our problem in seeing the picture that He's drawing for us, is twofold. The first problem is that the only sheep most of us have ever seen up close is in the petting zoo. And related to that is the fact that I doubt that any of us here have ever met a shepherd, much less talked to one. And the second problem is that few of us can see the picture He drew when He declared Himself to be the good shepherd whether we have seen sheep or shepherds or not.

My earliest image of the good shepherd comes from children's bibles, sunday school posters, stained glass windows—especially stained glass windows, the good shepherd seems to be a very popular image for stained glass windows—and statues. And all of them show an individual dressed in what we all have come to imagine to be the garments of first century shepherds, carrying a lamb on his shoulders. It's an ancient image that goes back to the very beginnings of Christianity. It's a good image, it is much loved, but it is insufficient.

Years ago while wandering through an art museum I stopped before an image of our Lord Jesus Christ enthroned like a medieval monarch wearing beautiful robes and wearing not a crown of thorns but a crown of gold, and underneath the image was the title of the painting: The Good Shepherd. A picture really can be worth a thousand words, and when I saw that painting, I came to a much deeper understanding of our Lord's words than I'd had before.

The thirty-fourth chapter of the book of the prophet Ezekiel contains these words:

> The word of the Lord came to me. Son of Man, proph-
> esy against the shepherds (that is, the kings) of Israel.
> Prophesy and say to them, even to the shepherds, Thus
> says the Lord God, You shepherds of Israel who've been
> feeding yourselves! Should not shepherds feed the
> sheep? Behold I, I Myself, will search for My sheep and
> will seek them out. I Myself will be the shepherd of My
> sheep, and will make them lie down, says the Lord God.
> I will feed them with justice. (Ezek 34:1-2,11,15-16)

Behind these words, we can hear the words of the twenty-third psalm so loved, I'm sure, by all of us. When our Lord identified Himself as the good shepherd, He was declaring Himself to be the good king, that is, the Lord God Himself, Who had come to search for His subjects and to call them to Himself in order to lead them into His kingdom. He was declaring Himself to be the fulfillment of the prophecy found in the book of Ezekiel.

Today's Gospel forms the introduction to our Lord's discourse on the good shepherd, and it does require some explanation. Hear the word of the Lord.

> He who enters by the door is the shepherd of the
> sheep. To him the gatekeeper opens; the sheep hear
> his voice and he calls his own sheep by name and leads

them out. When he has brought out all his own, he
goes before them and the sheep follow him for they
know his voice. (Jn 10:2-4)

Now this is what that's about. It was usual at nightfall at the
time of our Lord, to bring a number of flocks together into
one sheepfold where they would be kept for the night with
someone acting as lookout. Then at dawn, the shepherds
would come back and open the sheepfold and each would
call his sheep, which would gather around and follow him
out of the pen, and he would lead them to pasture. This is
the picture the Lord has drawn, and the point is that we are
to listen for His voice, and we are to follow Him alone.

We are to heed His voice and follow Him alone because He alone can give us life and give it abundantly. All
others, He warns us, all others who call us to follow them,
come only to steal and kill and destroy. The good shepherd,
in contrast to all the others, lays down His life for the sheep.

We live our lives assaulted by the voices of those calling us to follow them, to become members of their flocks,
and in the midst of this cacophony there is the voice of the
Lord calling us to follow Him. We're confronted constantly
with a life and death decision.

Now there's nothing abstract about this, and you don't have
to cast your mind back to Palestine two thousand years

ago. In 1969, I was a graduate student in theology at one of America's most prestigious universities. The country and the world had gone mad and universities, their faculties and students, had become increasingly politicized and radicalized. One of my fellow students was a woman who wore ragged clothes and distributed a Maoist newspaper. Now there were plenty of garden variety Marxist-Leninists running around both in the faculty and in the student body—but no, this woman was a Maoist, which she proclaimed loudly. And at a large meeting of students and faculty, she got up and declared herself to be, moreover, a cultural revolutionary. She wasn't alone but she was the most vocal. It made an impression, and I later learned that her father was, yes, a New York stockbroker. (I always wondered if she bought those ragged clothes from her parents' housekeeper or something, you know?) Although she was pursuing a Ph.D. in Theology, the voice that she heeded was not the voice of the good shepherd but the voice of another shepherd, the so-called Great Helmsman, who was responsible for the deaths of tens of millions of his flock. Tens of millions of those who heeded his voice and followed him.

In 1969 not many of us understood what the Cultural Revolution was, or what a cultural revolutionary was. It was a ten year saga of mayhem, destruction, and death. And the cultural revolutionaries, the Red Guards, were at the forefront of the destruction of Chinese culture and civilization and the lives, not of tens of millions of people, but the destruction of the lives of hundreds of millions of people. Mao's Cultural Revolution began in 1966 with his call, and it ended in 1976. *Ten Years of Madness* is an oral history of Mao's Cultural Revolution, and in it, fifteen people—among them cultural revolutionaries and others who had experienced the revolution first hand—share their experiences. I'm going to quote one of them whose memoir bears the striking title, "The Dear Price of Worship." And now I quote from this woman's memoir.

> *Worship is the most dangerous adventure in the world.*
> *It amounts to a pledge of one's life....*

Think about that. As we are all gathered here this morning, do you conceive of yourself being involved in the most dangerous adventure in the world? You know, that's really what we're up to. You know, it seems very peaceful here, doesn't it?—on this most dangerous adventure in the world, that costs our life. This woman learned the truth and she knew what she was talking about, but she goes on.

> *Worship is the most dangerous adventure in the world.*
> *It amounts to a pledge of one's life. The person I worshipped most was Mao Zedong. And not only me. Go ask anyone of my generation who they worshipped when they were in their twenties.*

After recounting the horrors she and a billion other Chinese endured at the hands of their idol, she concluded her memoir with these most striking words, and again I quote.

The worshipped destroy the worshippers by killing their souls.

Of course, we don't have to go to China for examples of this; there are plenty closer to home. Marshall Applewhite convinced his flock that he had been sent by God. He founded a religion called Heaven's Gate. (Think about that in light of today's Gospel when our Lord says (Jn 10:7), "I am the gate of the sheep.") He taught that a spaceship was following the Hale-Bopp comet that was due to appear and that in order to reach the spaceship and evolve to a higher level of being, he and his flock needed to commit suicide. They did. On March 26, 1997, thirty-nine people ate poisoned applesauce washed down with vodka, truly a sacrament of death. They were found in a 9,000 square foot home right here in our own Rancho Santa Fe. They were young, affluent, middle-class people with university degrees.

Then there's the People's Temple which I'm sure many of us here remember. Jim Jones, a Protestant minister of a church in San Francisco, divinized himself and led his flock from San Francisco to Guyana and founded Jonestown, where 918 of them died at his hands after drinking poisoned Kool-aid. Those who declined to receive his sacrament were shot to death.

Nor should we forget Charlie Manson and his flock—to the best of my knowledge all still alive and well at our expense, unlike their victims.

I read once that during the National Socialist era in Germany, a Roman Catholic priest stood up at Mass and in his sermon said, "We have no other führer than Jesus Christ." (The German word "führer" means "guide.") We have no other guide, we have no other shepherd, than Jesus Christ. Someone, we don't know whether it was a member of his flock, or whether it was a police agent there to listen in, reported him and he was executed. He was executed because he told the truth in public.

There is only one good shepherd, only one good king, only one true and living God, Who has laid down His life for us, and Who does not poison us but feeds us with His Own body and blood so that we can share in His Own eternal and abundant life. Only one good shepherd Who can lead us through this world to the kingdom of God. All others, without exception, are pretenders who have nothing to offer anyone except death. That's what our Lord is trying to tell us, that's the picture He's trying to paint for us. Our Lord, Who is enthroned at the right hand of the Father, where He lives ever to make intercession for us, I am certain prays that we will get the picture.

Amen.

PART IV

Perseverance

It's Happening Again

In the prayers of the diocese, there was nothing about the massive persecution of Christians by ISIS. You know, the diocese sends out these intercessions, right? You know we say, "in the diocesan cycle of prayer"…? I remember that there was no prayer for fathers on Father's Day! No mention of fathers. And today, given everything that's been going on in Iraq and Syria, no mention of Christian persecution, you know? So I'm thinking like, I'm suffering déjà vu all over again.

I saw this during the cold war, that the churches were silent if not complicit in the persecution of their own people in communist countries. The clergy of all the churches was riddled with communist sympathizers and unilateral disarmament people and "can't we just have peace?" people. No mention of what they were doing to the Christian faithful in those places — murdering them and enslaving them.

So all those years at my old church we prayed for the people in the camps and we included the stuff put out by

Keston College in the newsletter. Nobody else would do any of that. "We don't want to touch that!"

There was this very nice fellow. He was an engineer and he knew people who knew people and they wanted to revive a theological journal — I'm trying to remember which one it was — and he had a couple meetings. He asked to be put on the mailing list of the different churches because he was trying to enlist support for this. So I put him on the mailing list. I saw him a couple of years later and he said, "your newsletter is good. I like to read it." He says, "But you gotta forget that political stuff." And I said, "What political stuff are you talking about?" And he said, "You know that stuff about the Soviet Union." The Keston College thing I would put in. To him, that was just political stuff. I said, "Wait a minute! This isn't political, those are our brothers and sisters in Christ being tormented and imprisoned, enslaved for decades and killed and everything. That's not political stuff, that's… we need to remember them."

"No. That's just politics."

And then when the Rotary, the local Rotary Club invited me to go speak to them. I don't know what they thought I was going to say. It was kind of like… I guess they were inviting all the clergy on different days to come and it was my turn. And I belonged briefly to the Rotary back east because of my predecessor, I got sucked into it. So I'm thinking this is the Rotary, right? They're small businessmen, businesspeople. And clergy often join up. It's a service organization. And actually it was kind of life changing for me because back east, I went and the pastor of the Carpatho-Russian Greek Catholic Orthodox Church in America church, St. John the Baptist, who was a couple of years older than me, was there. And I met him and we became friendly and he introduced me to Schmemann. He had a wife and a couple little girls and invited Dorothy and me down to his place for dinner and we really liked them, it was really interesting and fun for us. Then he moved to a parish in New Jersey and we never saw them again. But even though there were Orthodox churches everywhere in Pittsburgh, they never had anything to do with the rest of us. So through him I got introduced to Orthodoxy and all that stuff.

So anyway I go to this Rotary thing and I do my dog and pony show on Keston College and you know, the book-lets with all the addresses of the victims in the camps and everything. And I say, "we can't do anything about their plight but Fr. Bourdeaux from Keston College points out that it's important for the authorities there to know that we know that they have these people. And so my parishioners and I send Christmas cards and Easter cards to them. And I'd like to highly recommend this to the Rotary as a good project." Honest to God, this was probably 1984, and their thing was "They're very powerful. They have nuclear weapons and we need to get along in the world." This is exactly what they told me. And it was all fear. "Oh, we wouldn't want to do that." Of course, I couldn't get any of the other churches interested, to do anything, you know? And I saw then how apt was Solzhenitsyn's story... he mentions more than once how Lenin is haranguing the comrades and he says we have to hang all the capitalists. And one of the comrades says but where will we get enough rope? And Lenin says don't worry, the capitalists will sell it to us.

Okay, I lived through all that. Now I'm seeing exactly the same thing. Silence about Islam. Covering up, excusing them. You know they said Stalin wasn't a real communist. Communism's really a good thing, you know? Mao? Pol Pot? No, they're not real. Communism's a wonderful thing. They're not real communists. Now we hear, oh, those people aren't real muslims. Muslims are wonderful people. It's a religion of peace, et cetera, et cetera. They're always fanatics or militants. No! This is just muslims being muslims.

So when I celebrated mass today, I said:

The most holy sacrifice of the mass is being offered to the greater glory of God and with special intention for all the victims of the Islamic State of Iraq and Syria, most especially for our brothers and sisters in Christ, the members of the ancient churches of those countries who are being murdered and enslaved and told to deny Christ and submit to Allah and his prophet or else flee for their lives. We need to remember them today and every day and ask God the Father, Who sees them as His adopted sons and daughters in God the Son Who dwells in them and suffers with them and for them, to grant them supernatural courage and heroic faith.

So said I.

13

The Usual Advice

In the name of the Father, and of the Son,
and of the Holy Spirit.

You therefore must be perfect as your heavenly Father
is perfect.

Mt 5:48

A couple of weeks ago I read an interesting article — interesting to me at least — by the New York Times columnist David Brooks. You may have read his book that lifted him from anonymity, *Bobos in Paradise*. He begins his column this way:

> *There is a strong vein of hostility against orthodox believers in America today, especially among the young. When secular or mostly secular people are asked by researchers to give their impressions of the devoutly*

faithful, whether Jewish, Christian or other, the words that come up commonly include 'judgmental, hypo-critical, old-fashioned (that's the lowest blow!) and out-of-touch.'

Mr. Brooks goes on to declare, "It's not surprising." There is a yawning gap, he claims, between the way many believers experience faith (you will notice he doesn't say "experience God" but "experience faith") and the way that faith is "pre-sented" to the world.

Note this bit of journalistic sleight of hand here. He does not say, or refer to how the faith is perceived or re-ceived by the world, but how it is presented to the world. And by this he means that we Christians (and although he mentions Jews and mysterious others, his column is meant for us, to instruct us Christians, as becomes clear if you read the whole article), he means that we Christians are failing to present our faith in a presentable and attractive manner.

And so he proceeds to give us a little homily on the horrors of conventional religiosity and then some tips on how we Christians — again not Jews or those mysterious others but how you and I — should behave so as to merit the approval of the secular and mostly secular people who find us so wanting.

Now, I have spent a lifetime, and it's getting to be a rather long lifetime I'm happy to say. I've spent decades and decades and decades from childhood on, listening and listening carefully to those Mr. Brooks describes as secular and mostly secular. A lifetime listening to them share their views and opinions about Christians and Christianity. And what I have learned from all that listening through all those decades — and here I'm erring on the side of charity, I really am — what I've learned is that there is an incredible indifference to God and to serious ultimate matters, compounded often by an abyss of ignorance, resentment, hostility, and unfounded prejudice.

And this hostility to and ignorance of Christianity and of Christians has been routinely and regularly presented to everyone on television and in the movies for the last half century. Day in and day out, week after week, month after month, year after year, we are presented by Hollywood in the worst possible light.

Dorothy and I have a joke between us. Well, we have a lot of jokes between us actually, but I'll share this one with you. I am a devotee of the murder mystery. I like to read mysteries, I like to watch television versions of mysteries, I love movies, you know, mysteries, murders, mayhem. And what Dorothy and I have noticed over the last decades is that if a character in one of these dramas on television or in the movies is wearing a cross, that's the murderer. You can almost count on it, the suspense is over. If they have a cross on the wall? Ugh, they're mass murderers. Serial killers!

And even if they're not the guilty party, they are so repellent, you hope they get arrested anyway. This is not a joke! This is how you and I are portrayed in the media relentlessly.

Now we are susceptible, if we are self aware, we are susceptible to almost any and all criticism of ourselves because we know, if we are in touch with the Lord and with our faith in Him, that as the great saint of the New Testament, St. Paul tells us, "we have all sinned and fallen short of the glory of God." (Rom 3:23) And every one of us can accuse ourselves of our faults and failings, our sins and iniquities, our faithlessness. And so whenever we suffer these criticisms it's easy to say, you know, "Gee, when I look at myself and I look at the faults and failures of the church, I'm guilty."

Time and again, therefore, in my lifetime, there is the notion that if we could just be more faithful Christians, more devout disciples of Jesus Christ, nicer people, then everybody would like us and approve of us and we'd get good press.

Time and time again, therefore, I've watched the churches and all denominations seek ways to make the world like us by good marketing. Hm? We live in a world where everything's marketing, right? Everything is overcoming sales resistance. If we could just market ourselves! If we could just convince people of how nice we are! Then they would approve of us! They would like us! And they might even come and join the church and gather around the altar with us. And there's enough truth in that to make it plausible...

But it's not true.

é

Two centuries before the coming of the Christ our Lord Jesus, the book of the Wisdom of Solomon was written. And in that very beautiful book which unfortunately the churches of the 16th Century Reformation excluded from the biblical canon, which I consider a great tragedy because it is a most important and I believe inspired work, inspired by the Holy Spirit, we read this:

> The unrighteous conspire together against the good man saying, Let us lie in wait for the righteous man for he is inconvenient to us and he sets himself against our way of life. (Wis 2:12)

That is a prophecy of Jesus Christ our Lord, the perfectly good man. And they conspired against Him because He set Himself against their way of life.

Two centuries after the coming of the Christ, when Christians were few in number and the church was absolutely powerless, the Christians were mercilessly persecuted in an attempt to utterly destroy the faith and the church. An anonymous Christian commenting on this unjust and unprovoked assault on the faithful wrote:

> The flesh hates the soul and wars against her without provocation because she is an obstacle to its own self-indulgence and the world similarly hates the Christian without provocation because they are opposed to its pleasures.

But there's more to it than that.

The church has faults, just as every Christian does, but that's not why the church has enemies. The church has enemies because it is the locus of the divine presence. The church has enemies because it is the temple of the Holy Spirit and the continuing tangible presence of Christ in time and space. And it is the Christ Who is rejected.

We Christians have an exemplar. There is One Who is perfect, and that's our Lord Jesus Christ, Who calls us to share in His perfection and Who today tells us that we ourselves must be perfect as He is perfect so that we can be sons and daughters of God the Father. Now this is both a call to imitate the Lord and also an apparent impossibility.

All that the Lord says in today's gospel that we are to do, is what He Himself did in His earthly ministry among us. (Mt 5:38-48) He was the One Who turned the other cheek when He was struck. He was the One Who was stripped of His garments by evil men and did not resist them. He was the One Who loved His enemies as well as His friends and prayed for them who persecuted Him even as they were torturing Him to death. He did not resist the evil men who attributed His ministry and saving work to the devil and murdered Him under the cover of both Mosaic and Roman law. Today's gospel is all about the Lord, His mission from the Father, and a description of His passion and death.

And He calls us, His adopted brothers and sisters, to imitate His example as Christian martyrs have done beginning with St. Stephen who while being stoned to death prayed for those who were murdering him.

The cross, the universal symbol of Christianity, is both a symbol and sign of God's love for the world *and of the world's rejection of God.* The paradox is this. The more faithful we are, the more we grow in holiness, the more we are conformed to Christ... the more we will suffer rejection, for we will share in the world's rejection of Christ Who was hated not because He was evil, judgmental, hypocritical, old-fashioned, or out-of-touch, but because He was perfect Goodness embodied in time and space.

And so our Lord tells us this. "This is the judgment," He says, "that the light has come into the world and men loved darkness rather than light because their deeds were evil." (Jn 3:19) And again He says to us, His brothers and sisters, "If the world hates you, know that it has hated Me before it hated you." (Jn 15:18)

The church has enemies not because of its obvious faults but because it is the locus of the divine presence, the God that the world wants to be rid of.

The Lord did not endure all that He endured at the hands of evil men because He was weak and passive and wants us to share in His weakness and passivity. He endured all because He trusted in God the Father. Specifically, He trusted in the Father's justice. He trusted that He did not need to vindicate Himself against His enemies, but that the Father would vindicate Him. When He calls us to imitate Him, He is calling us to share in His perfect trust in the Father's justice, the God Who declared, "Vengeance is mine, and recompense." (Dt 32:35)

And that's a verse from Deuteronomy that the apostle Paul quotes for us, the disciples of Jesus Christ, in his letter to the Romans. (Rom 12:19) And again the Lord says, "I will take vengeance on my adversaries and will requite those who hate me." (Dt 32:41) And again, "Praise his people, O you nations, for he avenges the blood of his servants and takes vengeance on his adversaries." (Dt 32:43)

And all of this is a truth that the church in my lifetime has been almost totally silent about. Silent about the justice of God, which God promises: an absolute justice.

Into Your hands I commend My Spirit

says our Lord, knowing that He does not need to enforce justice. The Father will do it on His behalf and on behalf of all who belong to Him.

And this is well understood by the apostle Paul again, who in today's reading from Corinthians tells us, "Do you not know that you (the faithful) are God's temple and that God's Spirit dwells in you?" (1Cor 3:16) As I've been saying, we are the locus of the divine presence. God wills to be tangibly present in the world through His union with us. Through His abiding in us, we are the body of Christ extended through time and space until He returns in glory.

> Do you not know that you are the temple of God and that God's Spirit dwells in you? If anyone destroys God's temple, God will destroy him. For God's temple is holy and that temple you are.

Making the faith pleasant and nice and acceptable to the world means abandoning Christ and His cross. Or as St. James puts it, (Jas 4:4)

> Friendship with the world is enmity with God.

And as for being perfect as our heavenly Father is perfect, this is clearly not a command because we could never ever fulfill such a command. It is rather a promise. The Lord has created us and recreated us through the grace of baptism to share in the perfection of His Son. He has created us to be perfect sons and daughters in His only-begotten Son. And that which we cannot possibly do, God promises to work in us because as the archangel said to the Blessed Virgin Mary, "With God nothing will be impossible." (Lk 1:37)

"Beloved," St. John tells us,

> we are God's children now. It does not yet appear what we shall be but we know that when He appears, we shall be like Him, for we shall see Him as He is, and everyone who thus hopes in Him purifies himself as He is pure. (1Jn 3:2-3)

Amen.

14

Food for the Journey

*In the name of the Father and of the Son
and of the Holy Spirit.*

Arise and eat, else the journey will be too great for you.

1Kings 19:7

On the ring that holds my church keys, I have a dog tag. It wasn't issued by the military. I received it from the Willoughby-Eastlake School District, east of Cleveland, when I was in the sixth grade. It was the height of the cold war and people believed there would be an inevitable nuclear holocaust caused by the arms race between our own country and the Soviet Union. The dog tag was issued so that I and my classmates, or at least our remains, could be identified when when that dread day came.

Some of us will no doubt remember Nikita Khrushchev, the Soviet premier, pounding a table with his shoe and screaming that dialectical materialism and international socialism, of which he was the leading representative at the time, would bury us. At the time we heard that, it sounded like a real possibility, and it was a chilling moment.

Things turned out otherwise, as we know. The Soviets were defeated by us and by the internal contradictions of Marxism. And in 1989, that evil empire—and it truly was an evil empire—collapsed, victim of a far superior adversary.

I carry my dog tag as a reminder of the cold war and its outcome, and also as a reminder that no one can read the future. The victory brought euphoria, at least among those of us who recognized that the Soviet Union was not one bit better than Nazi Germany, and we looked forward to universal peace and love. Do you remember that? We were going to have a peace dividend! How old do you have to be to remember these things? They seem so long ago now, hm? We were going to save all that money we were spending on defense. We were going to be using it for other wonderful things. Remember that? We had won!

But before the victory celebration was even concluded, an ancient enemy long thought to have been definitively defeated arose out of the ashes of the cold war and resumed its historically relentless attack. I'm speaking of course of a reinvigorated and ever-militant Islam. The Berlin Wall was torn down in November of 1989 and on February 23rd 1993, just a little more than two years after the Berlin Wall was demolished, Muslim jihadis detonated 1500 pounds of explosives which they left in a van in the underground parking lot of the World Trade Center Towers. They killed six people including a pregnant woman and her unborn child, and they injured a thousand more. Their plan of course was to bring the World Trade Center Towers down to the ground. They did a lot of damage and they killed people, but they didn't succeed. Nevertheless, eight years later, they succeeded, completely destroying the World Trade Center Towers, killing 2996 people and injuring more than 6000. 1993 and September 11th mark the dawn of the latest threat to western civilization in general and our own country in particular.

We're all reeling from the depredations of James Holmes and the drunken white supremacist in Wisconsin, but in an eerie convergence, the trial of Major Nidal Hassan, military psychiatrist at Fort Hood and Muslim jihadi (and you have to think about that: a Major in the American military, a medical doctor and a psychiatrist and a Muslim jihadi)… His trial has finally begun. As you may remember, in 2009 Nidal Hassan, screaming "Allah is great" murdered thirteen people and wounded 32 more. Hassan's trial is being delayed because the Major refuses to shave off the beard he has grown in violation of military regulations, to express his Muslim faith and identity.

Do I feel safer than I did when I got my dog tag in sixth grade? Not a chance.

ℓ

The world progresses and it regresses; it moves forward and it moves backward. Universal inevitable progress and the perfectibility of man is a myth, an invention of the Enlightenment of the 18th century meant to replace Christianity. And although it's a myth and a fraud, it is a most seductive myth. It has long ago infected the church itself, the one institution that should know better.

In 1907, to give just one example, Walter Rauschenbusch, known as the father of the social gospel and an enormously influential theologian, called on Christians to place their faith in the "immense latent perfectibility" of man.

The first and second world wars are often said by people writing history books to have brought such nonsense to an end, but the truth is, they haven't. And they didn't. And this seductive myth continues to permeate our lives. The truth is that things get better and things get worse. We take a step forward and we take another step backwards.

Consider television. I know, I always like to complain about television. But think about this. My flat screen high-def tv hooked up to the cable is a marvel of high tech. Right? It is! You can count the pores on the face of your favorite actor, or the hairs on his head, if he has any. But the programming is horrible. I often say to Dorothy that we've got 90 channels but nothing to watch. The content of the most seemingly innocuous programs is often vile. Primitive television with all its snow and flipping picture and all the rest of it, was banal and often attacked as mindless, but at least you could allow children to watch it without fearing for their morals, mental health, and immortal souls. And that's a fact.

Or take one of the truly great marvels of our age, medical science and technology. I am profoundly grateful for the great advances that have been made in medical science and technology. In fact, I'm here with you alive in this world because of advances in medical science and technology. And my wife, who is a cancer survivor, is definitely alive and well in this world because of advances in medical science and technology. But I also know that medical science and technology have reached the point where it can, in the trenchant phrase of C.S. Lewis, abolish man himself through genetic manipulation, cloning, and other grotesqueries. And while the technology and science has advanced marvelously, what about the profession itself? I would argue that it was a much healthier profession when doctors were bound morally, professionally, and legally by the Hippocratic oath.

In truth, I sometimes feel a bit like Elijah in today's reading from Kings, or at least I understand him. Elijah had triumphed over the priests of Baal, the Canaanite fertility god. The evil king Ahab and his equally evil wife Jezebel had lured the Israelites, who were all-too-willingly lured, into gross idolatry and worship of a false god. Elijah received from the Lord a great victory over the priests of Baal and over their idol, but it was short-lived. No sooner had Elijah vanquished and killed the 450 priests of Baal when Jezebel sent word to him saying, "so may the gods do to me and more also if I do not make your life as the life of one of them by this time tomorrow." Then Elijah was afraid and he arose and went for his life. And that's when we pick up the story today in the first reading that we heard from the book of Kings. (1Kings 19:4-8)

Elijah went a day's journey into the wilderness, and came and sat down under a broom tree; and he asked that he might die, saying, "It is enough; now, O Lord, take away my life; for I am no better than my fathers."

But then in the midst of this terrible discouragement and in the midst of this lament, when it appeared that everything was lost again, the Lord spoke to him saying, "Arise and eat." Bread and water appeared and, so nourished, he set out under obedience for forty days and forty nights to Horeb the mount of God.

Horeb is another name for Mount Sinai where Moses met with God, where Israel entered into covenant with God, and where the Lord Himself led Israel as they set out for the promised land.

In today's gospel, our Lord tells us that He is Himself tangible bread and living water. "I am the bread of life. He who comes to Me shall not hunger. And he who believes in

Me shall never thirst." (Jn 6:35) Those who first heard these words scoffed at them, as some have done ever since. And He said to them, "Do not murmur among yourselves." (Jn 6:43)

If you know your Old Testament, you'll know that Israel murmured against the Lord in the wilderness, saying that the Lord had not freed them from Egyptian slavery for their welfare, but to starve them to death in the wilderness. (Ex 16:2-3) Of course, the Lord did not starve them to death in the wilderness, He provided for them the manna, the mysterious food from heaven. But as our Lord points out, although the manna sustained Israel for a time, in the end they all died.

> Truly, truly I say to you, He who believes has eternal life. I am the bread of life. I am the living bread which came down from heaven that a man may eat of it and not die. (Jn 6:47-51)

℘

The world gets better and the world gets worse. Life improves and life declines. And in truth for all its beauty, this world is a wilderness. When the Lord says, "follow Me," he is asking us to trust Him, to believe that He is the way and that He knows the way, that He knows the way through the wilderness of this world. He knows the way even through death itself, and He is leading us to the land of the just, to his kingdom of eternal glory. And to sustain us on our journey, He offers us Himself, tangible food and drink, the bread of heaven and the cup of salvation.

And the word that the angel of the Lord addressed to Elijah is addressed by our Lord Jesus Christ Himself to us. Arise and eat, else the journey will be too great for us.

Amen.

15

All the Difference in the World

In the name of the Father, and of the Son, and of the Holy Spirit.

I'm a devotee of the mystery novel. I've been reading them all my life, or at least from early childhood, beginning with boys' mysteries, graduating to Sherlock Holmes, and from there to numberless other authors. I particularly love atmospheric mysteries set in places that I'll probably never get to visit. And I'm currently reading *The Tattoo Murder Case*, a 1947 classic by the great Japanese mystery author Akimitsu Takagi. Good stuff!

For years, I kept this to myself as a kind of guilty secret, something like watching daytime tv, or being a wrestling fan. Not that there's anything wrong with that! My grandmother and my wife's grandmother loved those wrestlers, you know. Gorgeous George. Some of us remember him. Almost fondly.

One day while visiting a priest friend of mine, a number of years older—a man for whom I have great respect, a learned man—I noticed by the door a stack of books waiting to go back to the library. Murder mysteries. And I realized that in him there was a kindred spirit, and not only in matters of religion. And so I asked him, "Why do we love these stories? Why do we read them?" And when he told me the answer, I found it so compelling and simple that I was embarrassed that I had to ask.

The mystery novel can deceive us or fool us. Its characters and plots are, on the surface, an entertainment and a diversion and they often seem unreal, even to those who really enjoy reading them. I've often wondered what a real private eye makes of Philip Marlowe, Alex McKnight, or Amos Walker, to name just a few. Yet underneath the fiction and the fantasy there is reality and truth. And that's what my friend explained to me.

The mystery novel—most particularly the murder mystery—is built on a firm understanding and acknowledgement of the reality and immutability (that is, unchangeability) of the moral order. The reader understands that a transgression of the law, most particularly the moral law, has occurred. And that the malefactor must be discovered and brought to justice if at all possible. I should point out that one of the greatest works of literature, Dostoevsky's

Crime and Punishment, is a murder mystery. And the genre runs the whole gamut from that very very great work to the silliest books you'll ever read. No murder mystery (no good murder mystery anyway) can be written by a moral relativist. The moral relativists are busy writing fiction, truly fiction, because it's built on a lie.

Flannery O'Connor—one of my favorite people in literature, and a Christian who understood the immutability of the moral law, and whose characters regularly transgress it to their everlasting shame and detriment, and to the detriment (of course) of everyone around them—Flannery O'Connor wrote to a friend, "Truth doesn't change according to our ability to stomach it."

The moral law can be broken, it can be ignored, it can be denied (all of which always has consequences) but it can never be suspended, it never changes. It just is. Our Lord Jesus Christ said this clearly when He said,

> Heaven and earth will pass away, but My words will not pass away. Ever.

That last word is my addition just in case you were remembering the verse (Mt 24:35) and said, 'I don't remember the Lord adding that.' That's the truth that our culture can't stomach.

In the Bible, the book of truth and reality, just as in a murder mystery, the form in which the truth is conveyed can conceal while it also reveals. Just as the form of the mystery novel can conceal the rock of reality on which its built, so the literary forms by which our Lord proclaims the truth to us can conceal as well as reveal the truth He wants to convey. The parables are a primary example of this.

Today we heard the Lord proclaim the Parable of the Sower. I might add that He did not simply proclaim it to the great crowds gathered about Him by the sea. He lives, and He has just proclaimed it to us using the vocal cords of our curate. The framers of the lectionary, however, chose to leave out eight crucial verses that follow immediately on our Lord's proclamation of the Parable of the Sower. If you look in your bulletin, you'll notice that there are verses skipped.

The Lord proclaimed the Parable of the Sower to a multitude gathered about Him. And then He left with His disciples. And in private, they said to Him, "Why do You speak to them (meaning the multitudes) in parables?" And He said to them,

> To you it has been given to know the secrets of the kingdom of heaven. But to them it has not been given, for to him who has will more be given and he will have abundance, and from him who has not, even what he has will be taken away. This is why I speak to them in

parables, because seeing they do not see, and hearing they do not hear, nor do they understand. But blessed are your eyes for they see and your ears for they hear. Hear then the Parable of the Sower. (Mt 13:10-17)

And in private then, He explicates the parable, and that's the second half of what you heard today in the reading from the Gospel.

Here, you see, is truth—a difficult truth—for all who have ears to hear (that is, all who can stomach it). To be a disciple of the Lord, matters; it makes a difference, all the difference in the world. In fact it makes a life-and-death difference. Our Lord said, "Those who believe and are baptized shall be saved, but those who do not believe will be condemned." (Mk 16:16) Those who follow the Lord and listen to Him receive His blessing; they are blessed in ways those who will not listen to Him are not. Those who have ears but will not hear do not receive the secrets of the Kingdom of heaven. And this is true whether we find it disturbing or difficult or unjust or unfair. Doesn't matter, it's still true. And I suspect the framers of the lectionary left that middle section out, that crucial connection between the parable and its explanation, in order to make the word of God easier for you and for me to digest. But of course there's more to it than that.

The Parable of the Sower describes what is, it describes what is. It is a revelation of reality, even though clothed in the language of the ancient world, and every parish priest and pastor lives with this reality throughout his ministry. People appear and become filled with zeal for the Lord. If they're not baptized, they ask to be. If they're not confirmed, they ask to be. They receive instruction with enthusiasm and become active members of the church, often busy in the church for the welfare of the church. And many, I pray most, grow in the faith that they have received, and as the Lord says, bear fruit a hundredfold, sixtyfold, thirtyfold, and only the Lord God Himself can know how much fruit anyone bears. (That'll be revealed to each of us on the day of judgement.)

But there are others just as zealous, just as interested, just as eager, who persist for a time, perhaps even a long time, and then fade away and sometimes simply disappear. "What happened?" we ask ourselves. It's the kind of question, you know, Father Doran and I ask one another in the sacristy. "What happened?"

What happened? Where are they? Why aren't they here with the Lord and with us?

If we learn anything—Father Doran and I and all those like us—we rarely ever learn the truth. All we learn is that all that love for the Lord and His Temple the church has become indifference, coldness, and at worst sometimes even hostility.

140

Next May I'll mark the fortieth anniversary of my graduation from seminary, and I received a letter from a classmate
announcing a class reunion next spring, a reunion that I'm
certainly looking forward to. So I went to school on the east
coast and most of my classmates remained there and I called
my best friend from seminary to tell him that I was going to
be attending the reunion and that I hoped he was also going
to be there and how much I was looking forward to seeing
our class after forty years, and that I hoped that everyone
would come. And he said that he would be there and hoped
that a lot of people would come, too. But he didn't really
know how many people would show up because of all the
people from our class who had dimitted the ministry during these past four decades.

You see, it's not just parishioners who abandon the
Lord. I wonder how many of my devout and fervent seminary classmates—and we were all devout and fervent—who
have walked away from their altars and the people entrusted
to their care have also walked away from the Lord Himself
and have found something more interesting and more en-
tertaining to do on Sunday morning than praise the glory of
the Father in union with the Son and all those who belong
to Him?

Our Lord experienced all of this Himself. There's no
time to go into it but when you get home, read the sixth
chapter of the Gospel of St. John, and you will know that

this is the experience of the Lord in His earthly life and ministry, and the experience of the church from then till now and until the end of time. And it shouldn't surprise us because the Lord has told us all of it in the Parable of the Sower. And so while Fr. Doran and I may be disappointed, we should never be shocked (right?), but say, "Well, the Lord told us that this is how it is! This is reality."

And it would be easy to say, "Okay, I get it. The Parable of the Sower explains what we all see." It'd be easy, that is, to make all of this about other people, to make the parable about others, while failing to hear it as a cautionary word addressed to each of us. The risen and exalted Lord says,

Be faithful unto death and I will give you the crown of life.

Fidelity to the Lord is for life, this life and the life to come. And each of us must be vigilant, according to our Lord in the parable and its explication, so that nothing can take the word of the kingdom planted by Him in our hearts, from us. The word of the kingdom is our Lord Jesus Christ in His Own person. And to be separated from Him, to allow anyone or anything to take Him from us, is to lose the most important of all the important things of life. And that's the truth concealed under the quaint imagery of the Parable of the Sower.

Amen.

16

God Bless St. Michael's

In the name of the Father, and of the Son,
and of the Holy Spirit.

According to the US Department of the Census, 43% of US children live without their fathers, 90% of homeless and runaway children are from fatherless homes, 71% of pregnant teenagers lack a father, 63% of youth suicides are from fatherless homes, 71% of high school dropouts come from fatherless homes, 70% of juveniles in state-operated institutions have no father, 85% of youths in prisons grew up in a fatherless home. Fatherless boys and girls are twice as likely to drop out of high school, twice as likely to end up in jail, four times more likely to need help for emotional or behavioral problems.

Today is the feast of the Holy Trinity and, perhaps providentially, it is also Father's Day. And these two celebrations are not unrelated. What I just read to you is offered not to be depressing, although it has to be distressing. I offer it to you as a kind of shock therapy, a reminder of just how important our fathers are, how gravely important the vocation of fatherhood is, and how much gratitude we owe to our fathers.

The statistics just read point to a profoundly troubling fact, and that is the gradual disappearance of the father and the consequences of his absence. Last year, for the first time in the history of our country, a majority of our children born to women thirty and under (51%) were born out of wedlock. And this points to disaster for all of us, not least of all for the children born to those women.

I have a close friend of more than twenty years, a clinical psychologist who has worked with children and adolescents for more than forty years. He does evaluations of young people who are troubled and in trouble, young people referred to him by judges.

Once upon a time he told me he'd ask these children, "Are your parents married or divorced?" That's a standard and important question. But with time that question became irrelevant and he began to ask them, "Have your parents ever been married?" And then that question became irrelevant. And today he asks them, "Have you ever met your father?" And time and time again the answer is, "No." He's also told me that in forty years of clinical practice, he's never met one teenaged prostitute whose parents were married. Not one.

Truth about most things is in short supply but truth about the family and in particular the importance of marriage and of fathers, is almost nonexistent. We all know how important mothers are. But we have been in the process of forgetting just how important fathers are. And the truth is that fathers and fatherhood have been denigrated and mocked too often over the last fifty years.

In my own childhood, one of the most popular television programs was "Father Knows Best." I loved that show, watched it every week. My whole family did. I can't imagine a show like that ever being put on television today. Although I usually avoid watching such things, whenever I do I notice in the situation comedy of today, fathers are too often portrayed as bumblers, inept people who need to be put right by women and above all, children. This isn't a figment of my tortured imagination. A very intelligent friend of mine, a wife and mother of two sons, has shared with me her own dismay and disgust with the way men in general and fathers in particular are portrayed on tv and in commercials, so often portrayed as clueless people. Again, people in need of being set right by women and above all, children.

I don't know if you've noticed it but in movies and television, the wise people who need to educate fathers are the children. Ten year olds possessing all wisdom. If only their fathers could catch up! And there's a reason for this — which there's absolutely no time to go into!

Popular culture teaches every day and in every way.

Bookstores are closing everywhere, but we're told that the average American watches four hours of television every day. And we need to be able to read television and movies the way we once learned to read books.

At the end of the decade of dissolution, that is, the 1960s, Gloria Steinem, former playmate bunny and self-proclaimed feminist, was credited with opining that "a woman needs a man like a fish needs a bicycle." Gloria however, claims that it didn't originate with her, that it comes from Irina Dunn, an Australian, who was inspired by a philosopher who asserted that "Man needs God the way a fish needs a bicycle."

In 1993, Robin Williams made a very popular movie, *Mrs. Doubtfire.* It's considered to be very funny, but I had trouble being amused because I know how to read movies the way I know how to read books. And the message of the movie is clear. Fathers are okay and can be allowed in the house if they become sufficiently feminized, if they become women.

All of this has had a great effect on all of us and certainly has had consequences for the church and society. As we heard in the first reading, (Gen 1:1–2:4a) that very long, long reading which is so easy to not listen to because it goes on and on. In that first reading which contains the seed from which the entire Biblical narrative grows. In that first reading, marriage and the family, we hear, is a divine institution, the primal institution, the institution which precedes the fall of man and the institution on which all other institutions depend, most particularly the church, for the church is the family supernaturalized.

Consider if you will, with me, the following questions.

Who is Jesus?
  Jesus is the Son of God.

Who is God?
  God is the Father of Jesus.

Who is the Holy Spirit?
  The Holy Spirit is the spirit Who proceeds from the Father through the Son to us so that we can praise the Father in union with the Son in time and eternity. (That's what we call heaven.)

What is the name of God?
  The revealed name of God into which every one of us has been baptized is, as we heard in the gospel: Father, Son, and Holy Spirit. (Mt 28:16-20)

(God always transcends the categories of His Own creation but this is the name with which God has chosen to name Himself, and the name He has chosen to reveal His Own triune being. And for this name there are no substitutes.)

What is the church?
The church is the bride of Christ, the temple of
the Holy Spirit, and His body.

Who are we?
To quote St. John: Beloved, we are God's children
now.

That is, we are adopted children of God the Father through faith and baptismal incorporation into God the Son in His death on the cross. This incorporation is effected by the Holy Spirit Who uses baptism as what the church has always called the means, the means of the gift, the means of grace.

Jesus alone, Jesus only, is born the Son of God. We are all born creatures of God who can only become children of God through faith and baptismal union with Jesus the only-begotten Son. Only Jesus has the right to call God "Father." And it is Jesus alone Who has the authority to give us permission to call His God and Father, our Father.

We Christians do not call God "Father" because we are projecting earthly fatherhood onto God. That's an absurdity really, if you think about it. I have children and I love them more than my own life, I really do. And my children have always told me that they love me. But if there's one thing that they know better than their own names, it's this. I am not godlike. Hm? You may have noticed that yourselves.

Joachim Jeremias, the great German biblical scholar, has pointed out that in the Old Testament God is spoken of as "father" only fourteen times and only then as creator, never as ancestor or progenitor. If you've ever even picked up the Bible, you will know how much longer the Old Testament is than the New. In the four gospels alone, God is spoken of as "Father" over a hundred times. Jesus spoke of God as His Father. And Professor Jeremias points out, nobody has produced one single instance in Palestinian Judaism where God is addressed as "my father" by an individual person. Think about that.

The only prayer of Jesus in which the words "My Father" is lacking is the cry from the cross, "My God, my God, why hast Thou forsaken Me?" That's the only prayer of Jesus that does not contain the words "My Father."* It was this insistence on the part of our Lord on His identity as the unique personal Son of the God Israel knew as Yahweh, that led to His crucifixion. They said that He had made Himself equal to God, and indeed He had.

Jeremias goes on to observe that there is no doubt that the "Abba," or "Father," which Jesus uses to address God, reveals the very basis of His communion with God. And I would add, of our communion with God as well.

---

* See "Concealed and Revealed" p. 97

Forty years ago, church bureaucracies began sending me, and other parish clergy, letters asking us to limit our use of "Father" for God and suggesting substitutes. I found them all absolutely absurd. In 1983, the Division of Education and Ministry of the National Council of Churches commissioned and published an inclusive language lectionary. In this explicitly anti-Christian lectionary we find such strange locutions as this.

> For God so loved the world that God gave God's only child so that whoever believes in the child might not perish but have eternal life.

And there's this.

> No one has ascended into heaven but the one who descended from heaven, the human one.

The Father and the Son have disappeared. Have disappeared and been replaced by an impersonal other who has no name. George Orwell would understand.

Let me quote the authors of this assault on God, our sacred scripture, and our faith. "God" they assert,

> is not a father, any more than God is a mother or than life is a dream.

150

With these words they have denied Christ and the God Who sent Him. They have denied the entirety of the Christian faith and revelation.

> *By reading and hearing 'God the Father and Mother' or 'God the Mother and Father' we provide a metaphor for God which balances the more familiar male imagery of God with female imagery.*

But of course our Lord Jesus Christ was never speaking metaphorically when He said that God was His Father.

And why must this be done? Because

> *the image of God as Father has been used to support the excessive authority of earthly fathers in a patriarchal social structure.*

In other words, the aim of all this is clearly political. God must be banished so that earthly fathers can be put in their place. Or to put it another way, God the Father must become Mrs. Doubtfire.

And here I should add this so called inclusive language is being used to destroy the historic Christian liturgies as well as the Bible. And here is a reason to celebrate and treasure St. Michael's. St. Michael's has never ever succumbed to this. St. Michael's has guarded the integrity of the language of faith. And the integrity of our language is inseparable from the integrity of our faith and inseparable from God. How important St. Michael's is!

The church is the bride of Christ and His body, and it is the temple of the Holy Spirit. And God will not desert his church. And while the church is going through difficult times, it is churches like St. Michael's that have guarded and preserved the integrity of the language of faith and therefore the faith itself. It is such churches that are the seeds that will provide for the renewal and rejuvenation of the body of Christ, His bride and His temple.

Now, while much of what I've said may be disturbing, it's not meant to be depressing, it's just meant to describe our situation as honestly and frankly as possible, to describe where we are and how important it is to use the right language, and how important it is on this Father's Day to celebrate fathers and fatherhood. Fathers matter terribly. Fathers matter and our Father in heaven matters absolutely. Our heavenly Father is the source of our earthly fathers and while the two must not ever be confused, neither must they be separated. Today is a day to remember our earthly fathers with gratitude, and to remember that there is nothing better in life than to be taken into the communion of love that God has revealed Himself to be, and to be allowed, *to be allowed*, to call the Father of Jesus, our Father, in the power and unity of the Holy Spirit.

Amen.

Appendix

Prayer

Father, receive our prayers and our praise,
    our thanksgiving,
    our gift of ourselves.
You have given us everything;
    we offer ourselves back to You knowing
    that if we do not, we will be lost.

So receive us,
    receive our offering and our thanksgiving,
    our gratitude for all your goodness
    to us and to those we love.
And watch over us all and keep us all safe in your care.

Be with our families,
    be with our congregation,
    be with our friends and all who have been good to us.
And watch over us in Your love and grant us Your grace
    to live as Your adopted children.

We ask as always for the grace to live simply, chastely,
charitably and above all prayerfully before You.

We ask You to forgive us our sins,
  to purify us of all evil,
  to fill us with the light of Christ
  and make us a blessing to everyone we meet.

May they see Your beloved Son in us, and may *You*
  see Your beloved Son in us.

May You see His face in our faces
  and our faces in His face,
  hear His voice in our voices
  and our voices in His voice.
And may He take our prayers
  and in the power of the Spirit
  perfect them in love
  and present them to You on our behalf.

For we ask all this in His name.

Amen.

Made in the USA
San Bernardino, CA
22 December 2016